FINDING GRACE IN THE GUTTER

> ONE OF THE BEST TRANSFORMATION STORIES I HAVE EVER HEARD
> DIMAS SALABERRIOS

g

JOSHUA KOTADINY

Finding Grace in the Gutter
Copyright © 2017 Uitgeverij Gideon
Copyright Nederlandse editie © 2016 Uitgeverij Gideon
Author: Joshua Kotadiny
Translation: Hanneke van Driel-van Dam
Editing: Helen Birkbeck
Cover photo: Paul Abspoel
Cover design: Margreet Kattouw, Studio Vrolijk

No portion of this book may be reproduced, stored in a retrieval system, or transmitted in any form or by any means – electronic, mechanical, photocopy, recording, scanning, or other – except for brief quotations in critical reviews or articles, without the prior written permission of the publisher.

Content

Recommendations
Three important lessons - Joël Voordewind — 9
Prologue — 11
1. America — 13
2. Back in the Netherlands — 17
3. Stoned — 21
4. King — 25
5. Robbery — 27
6. Violence — 31
7. 3 x 30 days — 37
8. Summer of 1994 — 43
9. From bad to worse — 49
10. Money — 55
11. The summer camp — 61
12. Mirjam — 69
13. Italy — 75
14. North Amsterdam — 83
15. Old friends — 87
16. A new life — 95
Epilogue by Ferry Kotadiny — 99
Acknowledgments — 101

Recommendation

"Joshua K. has one of the best transformation stories I have ever heard. You can see God's hand all over his life. You will not be the same after reading his testimony."
Dimas Salaberrios
Author of Street God, pastor of Infinity Bible Church New York

Three important lessons

"Joshua Kotadiny's life story takes us into the world of hustling gangsters, weed, alcohol, and crime. It brings to mind the harsh reality of the Bijlmer district, in which I grew up myself. Kotadiny describes in detail the growing gap between street life and his 'other world,' the Christian life. He was brought up with the truth and, being the son of an evangelist, was expected to set a good example. However, at a young age Kotadiny had already gone off the rails and chosen street life instead of a life with Jesus. In his darkest moments he eventually decided to return to the God of his parents. Just like the prodigal son, he came to his senses when all seemed lost. Then he started to develop a personal relationship with God.

Kotadiny's story contains three important lessons. The first one is about perseverance. Starting as a troublemaker, Kotadiny soon got entangled in the world of serious crime. In the eyes of the world this means you're lost and gone, with nothing more to expect than a life in and out of jail. God, however, didn't give up on him. Neither did his praying parents. Luke 18:1 urges us to keep on praying and never give up.

The second lesson we find in the Bible story of Martha. It must have been painful for Joshua's father to see his son choose the very life he had left behind. This story can be a wake-up call for us as Christians and as parents, and for me as a father. It is so easy to get totally absorbed by your work and to neglect your family at home, especially when you are a full-time minister. This is something which is hard to avoid, but it is not impossible. Martha's story shows us how we can lose ourselves in work and ministry. Just like Martha, we often get preoccupied with all sorts of things, while missing the most important. Kotadiny's story reminds us of the importance of applying the gospel to all aspects of our lives.

Joshua's compassion for drug addicts and homeless and criminal youths is the compassion of Jesus. Whatever we do for the least among us, we do for Him. We, as Christians in the West, are often too timid to express what matters most to us, while many people around us are in desperate need, without knowing the Heavenly Father who cares about them.

This book is nothing less than the gospel story of hope. When I joined Kotadiny one evening during an outreach, I witnessed his ability to bring this message across to the youths on the street. However, his story is more than just a personal testimony; it is a lesson for all of us: Keep on praying, don't get lost in your work, and always be ready to share the Hope living inside of you."

Joël Voordewind
Amsterdam, MP for the Christian Union Party

Prologue

It is January 22 and freezing cold. An icy wind blows across South-East Amsterdam's cemetery. I am standing next to the undertaker, who is visibly shaking, in spite of his long black coat and posh top hat. In fact, he is not shivering because of the cold; he is trembling with fear.

We are surrounded by hundreds of mourners, mainly men. Aggressive-looking men with tattoos, leather outfits, and bulging muscles. Together they are responsible for dozens of armed robberies, drug deals, rapes, and murders. They have served long prison sentences or still have many years in prison ahead of them. Without doubt, most of them are carrying a weapon. Hundreds of voices are chanting in a daunting cadence, "IR-ON MIKE! IR-ON MIKE!"

Iron Mike is the one lying in the coffin, which some men have just carried on their shoulders to the grave. Not in solemn silence, but with loud trumpet blasts and surrounded by a crowd of shouting people. Iron Mike has died after a shooting. I know him from the time I used to hang out on the street with his brother, Ponky. His relatives have asked me to lead the ceremony.

I have just made a speech in the cemetery's auditorium. All the guys from Bijlmer prison were there; my old friends and many members of the Crips Gang, from the Amsterdam and The Hague chapter. In front of these criminals and former inmates I spoke about Jesus. You could have heard a pin drop.

But now, as we stand around the grave, it is far from silent. The undertaker looks at me with panic in his eyes.

"You go ahead and finish," he sizzles, forcing the microphone into my hands. The next moment he's gone. Now what? Do I have to say something here, to all these shouting men? I try to think of something I can do. Pray! Isn't that what they often do at the end of a funeral? Often they pray, "Our Father"; shall I go for that, then?

"God, help me!" I silently pray. Then I grab a firm hold of the microphone.

"Gentlemen, silence, please! I want to pray with you for the bereaved!" I announce. To my surprise a hush falls over the crowd. Hundreds of eyes look at me expectantly. With my hands folded around the microphone, I take a deep breath and start praying. The words come straight from my heart. I pray for the family, the bereaved, but also for these men standing in front of me. I know from experience how hopeless their lives are, how wrong their decisions, and how strong the attraction of drugs and crime. But I also know the other option: a life with Jesus, in freedom and peace, with love and respect for and from others. From the depth of my heart I pray for the people around me.

After I've said "Amen," there is a moment of lingering silence. Then the crowd starts moving; some are going home, but many come to express their respect for the God whom I know. A seed has been planted in their hearts.

1 America

Before I was born, my father was a dangerous, drug-fueled criminal. After his conversion he became a passionate preacher and evangelist. My mother mainly looked after me and my elder brother and sister. She prayed a lot for us. My parents considered the "ministry," their work for God, as the greatest thing in life.

During the 1980's my dad met Pastor Sonny Arguinzoni, the founder of Victory Outreach International, who was working among drug addicts in Los Angeles. He held a crusade in the Netherlands and my father invited him to come and have a look at Amsterdam. He wanted to make him aware of the great need among drug addicts in the Netherlands. Arguinzoni came to Amsterdam and was deeply touched by the misery he saw. He challenged my father to come to America for training, so that he could start a church for drug addicts in Amsterdam.

My father accepted the offer and so we moved to America in 1985. My sister, Ravenna, stayed with an aunt but my brother and I joined my parents. My brother was nine; I was five. In Los Angeles we lived together with some other families in a property called a hacienda. Most of the people were of Mexican origin. Many of them had a background of drug addiction, but they had been set free through the ministry of Pastor Sonny Arguinzoni and were now serving God. As a family we lived in one room, in which all four of us also had to sleep. My brother and I shared one mattress. It was a pretty rough ride for all of us, but my parents really wanted to do God's work, even if it came with a high price tag.

My brother and I enjoyed the warm weather. We got up early every morning to catch lizards in the palm trees. We also had great fun in the swimming pool which we shared with our neighbors. Meanwhile my parents were busy all day, helping drug addicts and gang members from Los Angeles. They often took us along, so there was very little regularity in our life.

My parents didn't have much money. They got about twenty-five dollars a week to buy food, drink, and other essentials. My mother was often sad because she could not give us as much as she wanted. For example, there was no money for an ice cream on a hot day. As a small boy I could not understand this.

School wasn't easy either. I was the only dark-skinned child and was often called "Blacky" and excluded by the other kids. Many times I got blamed for things I hadn't done. Because I didn't speak English very well I wasn't able to defend myself, and I got punished unfairly.

As I wasn't able to express the anger this caused within me, I started fighting. I would kick and beat like mad. One time I even hit a boy neighbor from our hacienda with a belt till he bled.

My father was often away with Pastor Sonny Arguinzoni, or busy with the church. Caring for my brother and me was almost entirely left to my mother. My parents were struggling, being the only Dutch people in a strange country, doing difficult work in a hostile environment. My aggressive behavior really worried them and they tried to comfort me and pray with me. However, they were too busy with the ministry to look for another school for me.

After a few months things were getting better. We started feeling at home, people treated us more kindly, and we got a television set in our home. We also got two dogs, black pit bulls, which I was very fond of. During that time we also went to great theme parks and baseball games. At school and in our neighborhood, however, the bullying by other kids continued. I missed my parents' presence and support.

2 Back in the Netherlands

After ten months in America, we returned to South-East Amsterdam in 1985. As we did not yet have our own home, my grandmother allowed us to live in her house. Every Sunday there were church meetings in the living room. Initially it was only with the family, but gradually more people started to join in. As a young boy I saw this small gathering grow and become a church with 1500 members in the center of Amsterdam. My parents were working day and night for the sake of the gospel. Every day they shared the love of Jesus with the addicts on the Zeedijk (the street leading to the red-light district). Sometimes, when they couldn't find a childminder, they would take my brother and me with them. Till late at night they carried us on their shoulders while handing out tracts.

Meanwhile, the church had moved from my grandmother's house to a location near Dam Square. Hundreds of people were now attending. I remember one evening during which an altar call was made especially to drug addicts. My father and the other church leaders laid hands on the addicts and prayed for them. I saw grown men and women cry and, as a small boy, I was so touched by what my father was doing for the gospel that I ran forward. I laid my hand on the man my father was praying for (I only reached the height of his hip) and started praying along. I was about eight years old.

My father wasn't at home a lot, but when he was, he really tried to give me his attention. When I said that I wanted to learn to play the drums, he bought me a drum kit. When I asked him to take me to the cinema, he would do it as soon as he had time. He also took me to McDonald's or on walks through the city.

One day I told my father that I wanted to learn how to fish. When I came home from school, he surprised me with two fishing rods. Off we went together. In his old life, my father had been used to holding a gun; in his new life it was a Bible. A fishing rod, however, was quite another story. Within no time the fishing line had become a hopeless tangle, with no chance of catching a single fish. But I had such great fun! I will never forget that day.

I immensely enjoyed those times spent with my father. However, the restlessness which I had felt in America was gradually growing. I became unmanageable.

When I was about eight or nine years old, I started stealing. At first I stole computer games from my classmates' coat pockets and chocolate, crisps, and soft drinks from the supermarket. I did this together with some friends from our neighborhood.

On Friday evenings prayer meetings were held in the church. Dozens of coats would be hanging on the coat rack. Together with Gilbert, a Sunday-school friend who also lived in our neighborhood, I rummaged through the coats' pockets. We found cash, bank cards, and other valuables; apparently the church people had such a trust in their fellow church attendees that they left all their belongings in their coat pockets. For a few weeks we were able to carry on freely. But then an announcement was made from the stage that there was theft going on and people had to be more careful. No one knew that the son of the evangelist Ferry Kotadiny was stealing in his own church.

At school I wasn't doing well either. Owing to the time in America and the different language used there, I had fallen behind and was placed one grade back. This only added to my frustration and I started fighting even more. I rebelled against my teachers and threatened other kids with a pocket knife, forcing them to give me their lunch. One day I caused such chaos in our classroom that the teacher lost the plot and ran out. Another time my friends and I threw a brick through the classroom window. The next day the teacher said that this could only have been done by very bad children. "Well, then I am bad," I thought.

Every time I misbehaved, the teachers contacted my parents. They gave me a harsh telling off but it didn't make any difference; their words went in one ear and out the other. Over time I became insensitive to my parents' hurt and anger. We spent little time together as a family. Occasionally, my father did something nice with me. At those times he would do his best to be a good father and give me his attention. However, this was rather the exception, as it did not happen very often. I needed structure and continuity in my life, but these were difficult to find in our family and our church.

Meanwhile, we had moved from my grandmother's house to a place of our own in Gein, a neighborhood with lots of new-builds. It was a nice area with many families. My sister was living with us again. She was now sixteen years old and in the evenings she often sneaked out to the disco. Every day my parents were working for the gospel till late at night. (If my father did something, he did it 100 percent. That's how he had been when he was a criminal, and after his conversion it was still the same.) If my parents came home late from church or outreach and my sister was not yet at home, there was real tension in the house. When she came back late at night I woke up to the sound of my father's voice telling her off.

My brother and I were often home alone during the evening. We felt the unbearable tension: Month after month there was ongoing conflict. Then, one day, my sister did not come home; she had run away. My parents were desperate and searched everywhere: in the streets, in night clubs, at relatives' homes. Finally we found out that my sister had gone to my grandmother. She stayed there. From that time on our family was no longer complete.

   I saw my parents' grief. They worked so hard to share the gospel and to bless others, but at home they were dealt one blow after another. I could see the disappointment in my father's face but I did not know how to deal with it. I only got more rebellious. In the evenings I often hung out on the street with a group of boys who lived a few blocks away, in an area of mainly council housing. Many of those boys were growing up without a father. During our childhood we played outside, we played normal kids' games, but during summer evenings we also sneaked into the grounds of the local outdoor swimming pool to organize our own private swimming parties.

3 STONED

When I was about thirteen years old, I spent a lot of time with my two cousins. Our fathers were brothers; they were half-Moluccan, half-Austrian. Initially they were quite shy so I took them out onto the street to help them toughen up a bit. We nicknamed them Playboy and Bootje. Their mother used to smoke Berkeley cigarettes and we often took some with us to smoke together. I didn't like the taste at all but we thought it was cool to smoke, so we did it almost every evening on the street.

Another friend of ours was Klight, alias Kisri. He was a tall lad from a Surinamese background. He was very trendy and always involved in conning other boys in the neighborhood. One evening he came over to us with Merrel, a short, skinny Aruban guy, who was very good and quick at stealing. When they saw us smoking, they suggested going to a coffee shop downtown to get stoned. Andre, alias MC, a stocky Creole-Surinamese guy, joined us as well. MC was always backing me up in fights and was popular with the girls. He was a smooth talker and often managed to persuade the police officers to let us off the hook.

The six of us took off to Waterlooplein, to a coffee shop called "Smoesie." We bought a readymade joint (rolling one ourselves was still too hard) and went into a quiet alley. One by one we took a deep drag of the joint. Kisri and I started coughing, and

MC was having trouble too. Soon, however, we got a kick and started laughing; we were seeing everything double. We took the underground back to Gein. MC got so stoned that he could no longer feel his feet. Nevertheless, we had gotten the taste for it and from that day on we went to Waterlooplein every day to get stoned. More guys joined us: Lewi, a boy who didn't want to smoke but liked to come along; he was very quick at stealing and robbery. And then there was Mauro, nicknamed Ponky, a handsome boy and a good footballer. His brother had spent several years in prison and was notorious in our neighborhood, so no one messed with Ponky. At a young age he was already drinking lots of alcohol on the street. I often sat drinking and smoking with these boys. On Saturday nights I usually sneaked away from home and went with them to the Leidseplein and Rembrandtplein in the inner city. We bought loads of weed and then went out to see what the night had to offer.

We were stoned as we boarded the underground or night bus. We often continued smoking on the underground, although this was prohibited. No one dared to stop us anyway. During the ride we made our own music: Beating a rhythm with our hands against the benches, we took turns at freestyle rapping, making up our own lyrics. The other people on the underground, who were travelling home from work, did not quite know what to do with us.

When the other boys in Gein saw the impact weed had on us, they wanted it too. They saw that we didn't worry about anything after we had had a joint. All problems were gone for a while. We all needed that; something that would help us not to think about our lives at home.

When I came home stoned, I would quickly run upstairs to wash my face, brush my teeth, and spray on some deodorant, so my parents wouldn't find out that I had been smoking. I think my parents knew anyway, because my father had been on the streets himself. However, he was too busy with the church ministry and not often at home. My mother was around but didn't pay too much attention. Sometimes she caught me doing something crazy but she didn't realize how far I had gone. I lived in two separate worlds: one out on the street, where it was wild and dangerous, and one in a safe, Christian environment, in which I felt God's presence.

At home I sensed a peace which stood in contrast to the restlessness I was feeling inside of me. The street was drawing me like a magnet and I kept going back to my friends. Although I appreciated the way my parents had brought me up, I chose street life. I did not want to hurt my parents and pretended that I was following their rules. By doing so I gave them hope, but it was a false hope.

On Sundays my parents often spoke in other churches. We had agreed that I would attend our church in Amsterdam when they were away. I would leave home a bit earlier and say, "Bye, Mom and Dad, have a good time; I'm going to church!" I would leave the house wearing my church outfit, but instead of going to church I hid behind a fence at the end of the road. I waited till my parents had gotten into their car and driven off and then I went back home. I quickly changed and put my street outfit on – Nikes, Chipie trousers, Australian sweater, and my Nike cap. Then I ran to MC's house. MC opened the door, still half asleep and wearing only a pair of boxers, and asked me why I had come so early.

"Hey, dude," I said. "My parents think I'm in church, but I don't want to go. Can I chill out here?"

MC wasn't fully awake yet. "Bro, it's only half ten; my mom wants quiet in the house on Sundays. But you can chill in the porch if you want." And that's what I did: I sat in the porch with a joint or a cigarette till my mates were ready to go and hang out on the streets.

At school things were going downhill too. I skipped many school hours and when I was in the classroom I wasn't paying attention. Eventually I was expelled.

At the next school I broke into the canteen and stole food and drinks. They sent me away as well. I went to another school, where I got caught having sex with a girl in the toilets. I was sent away yet again. My father got phone calls from the school directors and had to come in for talks. Afterwards he gave me full-blown sermons at home but his words bounced off me.

I had no clue what I was doing to myself. I was constantly drunk or high on weed. For months in a row I didn't go to school and I spent more time on the street than at home. I told my parents that I was attending school, but in reality I was hanging out with my friends. Stoned and drunk, we staggered through the streets, always on the lookout for things to "hossle" (steal). I felt empty, lonely, and misunderstood. My mother was crying a lot and I knew that she was sad about my lifestyle, but I didn't have the strength to change it. My father was often away for church ministry. When he was at home, he talked to me about my behavior, but there was no spiritual connection between us as father and son. His approach didn't work; he didn't get through to me. I sought pleasure and relaxation on the street. That's where I at least felt a sense of belonging.

4 KING

At that time there were two boys' gangs in Gein: the G-Boys and the G4-Boys. The G-Boys were guys aged from eighteen to about twenty-three, who were involved in drug dealing, bank robbery, and gambling. I was part of the G4-Boys, a group of twelve-to-seventeen-year-olds, some of whom had already been sentenced for robbery, violent assault, stabbing, etc. We went from bad to worse and were stoned every day

There were fights within the group as well. When I was twelve years old, I once got into a fight with a boy from our group, whom we called Tjakkie. In the presence of my friends he had forced me to the ground and kicked me several times. I felt deeply humiliated. I am Moluccan and my name is Kotadiny. In the Moluccan community we were always told that we are real fighters. Besides, I had to defend the honor of my family; during the 70's, when my father and my uncles were notorious on the street, everyone knew that you don't mess with the Kotadinys. So I had promised myself to pay Tjakkie back. I wanted the whole neighborhood to see it so that I would be respected again.

When I was thirteen, I planned my moment of revenge. All my friends knew about it; I had asked them to round up all the boys in the neighborhood so they would see it happen. I wanted to make sure that I would win this time. Therefore, I brought along a knife and an air gun, the bullets of which I had sharpened. If I shot at his head, he would be badly wounded.

We stood facing each other. A group of about twenty boys had gathered around us, shouting and cheering.

I said, "Tjakkie, do you remember thrashing me?"

"I do, man," he replied calmly. "And I'll smash you to bits this time."

"If you touch me again, I'll break your back," I responded.

Tjakkie wanted to take off his coat, but that was a mistake. I seized my chance and attacked him. I pointed my air gun at his head and pulled the trigger... I missed! He saw what I was doing but I didn't give him a chance to attack me. I ran towards him and jumped on top of him. I hit him on the head with my air gun, one, two, three, four times. He got dizzy and fell to the ground. Blood was streaming from his face but I kept beating and kicking him, dragging him down the whole street. My vision blurred into a red haze as I kicked and beat him as hard as I could. "This is what you get back from me!" I shouted, as I punched him in the face.

"Take him away, take him away!" he shouted at the others, but no one dared to intervene.

I grabbed his collar and yelled in his face, "Who's the king? Say, 'Joshua is the king!'" I kicked him again.

He shouted in a frightened voice, "Joshua, you are the king!"

"Louder!" I screamed, and he shouted,

"Joshua is the king!"

At that moment, my cousins Bootje and Playboy joined in. According to the so-called family principle, they had to help me, so Tjakkie received some more kicks from both of them. Then the other boys pulled us apart.

From that day on I was well respected among the G4-Boys. Tjakkie stayed in the gang but he never touched me again.

5 ROBBERY

One evening, when I was still only thirteen years old, I was outside till the late hours. I was standing with a group at the basketball field and I heard some of the older boys talking about a plan for that evening. They wanted to break into a store that sold expensive equipment. I said to Lewi, "Hey, dude! Did you hear that? Man, let's join them!"

Slightly startled, Lewi said, "Josh, you're mad! Those guys are much older than us; they'll never let us join them."

But I said, "No, man! I want to go; let's join them and plunder the whole thing!" Then I simply walked over to the boys and asked if we could come with them. They started laughing and said,

"You better go home, kid; you're way too small for this sort of thing!"

"All right then," I said. I winked at Lewi and said, "Let's roll." Lewi understood right away and we got on the bikes we had stolen from the underground station and cycled through the streets of Gein in the middle of the night.

I said to Lewi, "You don't really think we're going home, do you?"

He grinned at me. "Are you crazy? Think of all the equipment we could steal from that shop!"

I slowed down. "If we go, we have to make sure they won't send us away."

Lewi suddenly slapped his hands on the handlebars. "Ponky!"

he exclaimed. "If we take that guy along to the robbery, those guys will leave us alone!"

I thought that was a good idea, but then I asked, "Isn't it too late to pick him up? He might be asleep."

"Haha," Lewi laughed. "Ponky is up for these things any time, bro." We went to Ponky's house and knocked on the door. Fortunately he was still awake and we told him that the big boys were about to rip off a shop. Ponky was immediately up for it and he came with us. We cycled towards the Reigersbos shopping center. My heart was beating fast as I thought about all the equipment we could get. At home we weren't swimming in money. There was always food, but as a teenager I wanted to have some proper equipment in the house. How cool it would be to have a sound system in my room! I also thought about being caught by the police. What would happen then? What would my parents think?

Once we arrived at the shopping center, I forgot my worries and fears. I flung my bike into some shrubs, paying attention to the exact place so I could find it quickly and get away after the robbery.

Lewi, Ponky, and I walked together to the shop. The other boys saw us coming. I could tell by their looks that they wanted to send us away but they didn't dare to because Ponky was with us. Ponky was a younger brother of Bietje, who had served a five-year sentence for sixty-four armed robberies. Bietje and his gang from Gein were the bosses of the block. In 1991 their photos had even been on the front page of the Telegraph, heralding them as notorious gangsters from Bijlmer. Because of this, the boys had respect for his brother, Ponky, and right now that came in handy.

It was three o'clock in the morning. One of the boys pulled a big concrete cutter out of a sports bag. He cut through the bottom part of the shutter and with about fifteen other boys we tried with considerable force to pull the shutter up. This caused a loud squeaking noise, which could easily wake people up. So, when we were halfway through, we stopped pulling and one of the guys told Luke to throw a stone through the window. Luke was a guy who drank lots of alcohol. He had a paving slab in his hand, which he flung straight through the window. The entire pane was smashed into pieces and we all dashed into the shop. We took everything we could lay our hands on. Luke and I grabbed hold of an expensive video player. As soon as I got my booty, I ran outside. But then I heard the wail of the alarm system. While running out I had probably touched something which triggered the system.

The other boys ran off as well; they all followed me as we made our way to our bicycles. With all the heavy equipment in our hands we weren't as fast as we would have liked to be. We heard the sirens of police cars getting closer. I saw Lewi and three older boys running next to me. As they ran, the older boys suddenly knocked the equipment out of Lewi's hands and picked it up. I saw that they wanted to take my stuff too, but I gave them a look which said I would kill them if they tried that. I didn't care how big they were; I wasn't afraid of them. So they ran away with Lewi's things.

"Bastards!" he shouted. I was shocked that boys from our own group, with whom we hung out on the street every day, could be so vile.

There was no time to think about this, though. The police were on our heels and we had to flee! We quickly took our bikes, I put my stolen stuff in the cycle bag, and together we started racing towards Gein. When we arrived, exhausted and sweating, Lewi suddenly said, "Ponky! Man, I hope Ponky hasn't been caught!" But a little way down the road Ponky was sitting waiting for us, laughing and holding a big stereo system in his hands.

We all went home and I put my bike in the shed. I kept the video equipment hidden in my cycle bag so my parents wouldn't see it. As I climbed in through my bedroom window I heard my mother praying in her room. Wow, she's a fanatic! I thought. It's four o'clock at night and she is still praying! I didn't pay much attention to it, however, and went to sleep.

6 Violence

When I was fourteen I got arrested for the first time. It was a quiet, late-summer evening in September and we were hanging out as usual with a group of boys in Gein's shopping center. There were about fifteen of us, all G-4 boys. Everyone was stoned and drunk. Anybody passing by got something flung at his head; either a nasty remark or a stone or a beer can. Most people quickly moved on. Till this giant guy came by and saw what we were doing. That tatta shouted that we had to stop, and stormed right over towards one of my friends, Lotje. He was one of the youngest in our group. I walked over to help Lotje, but the guy made a move as if he was ready to strike me.

Out of nowhere Ponky came flying past me and gave the guy a huge blow to the stomach. The man fell to the ground. He shouldn't have done that. Ponky and I started kicking and beating him like crazy things. We completely demolished him till the point where there was no more movement. Then Ponky stopped, but I continued. I just kept kicking his body. I was filled with a deep hatred of this man, although I did not even know who he was. The man fell into convulsions and foam started coming out of his mouth. His eyes were blinking and his pupils flicked back and forth. One of my friends felt in the guy's pockets and took his wallet. I gave the man one more kick in the head, so hard that I bruised my foot. I faintly heard someone yelling, "That guy is crazy!" but it did not bother me. The anger in me had taken over completely.

We quickly fled into a nearby alley, where we divided the contents of the wallet. There was some money and there were a few bank passes, including credit cards. The others were only interested in the cash, but I quickly slipped the credit cards into my pocket.

The next day I was still limping when I met my friend Mike on the street. He asked me what was wrong with my foot, and I told him what had happened the previous evening. I proudly demonstrated how we had wrecked the tatta and pinched his wallet. I added that my last kick had been so hard that I had bruised my foot.

Mike started laughing and asked me if I had anything else with me. I showed him the credit cards and together we walked to the ATM to see if we could get any money. The previous night I had been too drunk and stoned to try it, but now I had high expectations. Maybe I could get a big stack of money! The credit card had a code. I had never yet used such a thing, but I tried anyway. I put the card in the slot and typed in the code I had read on the card. It seemed to work! We could choose the amount we wanted to withdraw and stood bouncing with excitement in front of the cash machine. But when the money was supposed to come out, the cash machine indicated that the card was blocked. No transaction was possible. We were gutted!

The credit card came back out and I put it in my pocket. Maybe I could try again at another machine. That same evening I went downtown with a few boys to get weed. We went to Waterlooplein and rolled a joint. The five of us walked to the train station and were sitting down to chill when two police officers came by, a white one and a dark one. I was the only one blowing. The officers said it was forbidden to blow at the station and asked me how old I was. "I'm seventeen," I lied.

"Can I see your ID card?" the dark officer asked. I told him that I had unfortunately left it at home. Then I had to go with them to their office, which was nearby, at the train station. My friends were allowed to go because they had no weed.

At the office they subjected me to a proper questioning. They didn't believe that I was seventeen, so they kept asking me who I was. However, I stuck to my story. Then they asked if I had any other illegal stuff on me. I could easily deny that, because I had no other drugs or weapons with me. Nevertheless, they wanted to search me. In my back pocket they found some fluids and cigarettes and, to my horror, the two credit cards that I had taken with me. They saw that they had a Dutch name on them. Because of my skin color and because I did not have any ID, they sensed right away that this was fishy. I was handcuffed immediately.

There I sat in the police station, with handcuffs on. All sorts of thoughts were racing through my mind. Why had I been so stupid as to keep the credit cards in my pocket? What would my parents say if they were told that I had been arrested?

The officers kept asking me who I was and what my name was. I gave them all the boys' names I could think of and the men were getting angrier all the time. I kept playing this game for almost half an hour. I was scared to death, because I knew I was in serious trouble because of the credit cards. Undoubtedly the victim had already made a statement. I was hoping they would let me go if I pretended I was crazy.

The white officer was pretty nice but the dark man was much tougher with me. That struck me: I expected him to be friendlier because we were both colored. He was a stocky Surinamese guy with a big mustache and gray hair. I thought I knew the Surinamese people – after all I had grown up among them. But this man seemed to be a racist! I will never forget that ugly face, I thought. I can't stand him; what a color traitor!

After half an hour they gave up trying to find out my name. Instead, they started fishing for other information: What were my parents' details? They asked for phone numbers, so I gave all the phone numbers I knew: my aunt's, my neighbors'... They called them all but, of course, nobody knew the person with the false name I had given them. This also went on for a long time until the effects of the weed began to fade. I realized they would not let me go and that I would have to stay there overnight. It dawned on me that things were getting pretty serious. The police officers were starting to shout at me.

"Okay, I'll give you my real name and number," I said with a sigh. I hoped they would then let me go. I gave them my parents' phone number and the officer dialed it. I heard my sister answering the phone. The officer asked for my father. He was at home.

The agent held the receiver to my ear and I had to tell my father what was going on. With great difficulty I told him that I had been arrested because I was suspected of being involved in certain things. I kept it as vague as possible; I found it hard enough to pass this message on to my father. My dad did not say much, but I heard his voice tremble. He sounded like he was about to cry. Deep inside I was now feeling sorry for what I had done.

The officer took over the conversation and told my father that they would keep him informed of what would happen next. When we finished the phone call, I was taken, handcuffs and all, to a police van which stood ready to go. They brought me to the police station at the Central Station, where I was put in a cell.

I thought I'd have to wait there for a little while, till my parents came to fetch me. I felt alone and also a little scared, because I did not know exactly what would happen to me. My thoughts whirled in all directions. What if I was to be put in jail for months? What would my friends be doing? I missed their company; normally I was surrounded by friends from the street, but now that they weren't with me I felt lonely, small, and scared.

After a while (to me it seemed like hours), an officer entered my cell. I was happy because I thought I would be released. However, the officer had other news: I had to go to the police station at Flierbosdreef in South-East Amsterdam, where I would have to spend the night in a cell. That was a disappointment!

But I was too tired to really care. After all that had happened I could probably cope with one or two days at the police station. At midnight I arrived at the police office at Flierbosdreef. I was taken to a cell with a blue door with the number ten on it. Inside were a steel toilet bowl and a stone bed with a thin mattress and a dusty brown blanket.

Although I was tired, I couldn't sleep. I wondered what my friends would do if they were in my position. I had heard dozens of stories about their experiences with the police. The main rule was: "Keep your mouth shut at all times, and don't get too chatty with those blue blokes." So far I had stuck to that rule quite well, I thought.

Apparently I did fall asleep at some point, because around six o'clock in the morning I was awakened by an officer opening the hatch on my door. He put a coffee and a cheese sandwich down. I had tasted coffee before and never really liked it, but this coffee was definitely the most horrible I had ever drunk in my life. After forcing the sandwich down my throat, I had to refresh myself and prepare for interrogation.

My fingerprints and some photos were taken. In the interview room I sat once again facing two officers, who asked me how I had gotten those credit cards. I kept telling them that I had found them. They tried in all kinds of ways to get more information out of me, but it didn't work. Eventually they took me back to the cell.

I didn't have a watch, so I had no idea what time it was. In the ceiling was a small window, through which I could see a little bit of sky. So I knew if it was afternoon or evening, but beyond that I had no idea of the time. The first afternoon I didn't find it too bad sitting in my cell. After a few hours they came to pick me up again for another interrogation. I kept telling them that I had found the credit cards, and once more I was brought back to my cell.

The second day seemed to be never-ending. For hours I sat in my cell, feeling tired, lonely, and bored. In my mind I kept going over what had happened and what I could have done differently. I felt gutted about being locked up while my friends were walking around freely outside and angry with the police because they had arrested me. At that time, I did not realize the severity of what I had done. I didn't feel regret, only anger and loneliness.

The next day was the same. In the cell, minutes seemed like hours and I was tired and depressed. Up to now I had always maintained that I had found the credit cards, but it became clear to me that the officers didn't buy that. I gave up. I pressed the bell.

7 3 X 30 DAYS

The officer opened the hatch of my door and asked what he could do for me.

"I want to make my statement," I said listlessly. He took me to the interview room and called a colleague.

"Actually, you do not need to make a statement," he said, to my surprise. "Your friends have told us already what you've done."
I was furious. I had little experience with the police and I was exhausted after days in the cell. "They would never do that!" I shouted.

But the officer said calmly, "You better tell us everything, Kotadiny."

I was too tired to come up with any more lies. I told them what had happened.

"We were on the street with a group of boys and then we got attacked by a white man. One thing led to another and we got into a fight. In the midst of all this his wallet slipped out of his pocket and his credit cards fell out. I picked them up and ran away."

The officers probably realized that this wasn't the complete truth, but they accepted my story for now and took me back to my cell. I asked them what day it was. It was September 24. The birthday of my grandma Lies! She was turning sixty-five and I was going to do a rap for her, together with my cousin. At that moment I felt ashamed of myself. At the party, my parents would look bad in front of the whole family because I had been arrested.

Before I entered cell number ten, I looked through the open door of the cell next to mine. A stocky young guy in a black leather jacket was sitting on his bed. He greeted me and told me that his name was Achmed, and that he was in there for pickpocketing. That evening we kept talking through the slot in the cell door. He was Moroccan and came from a district in Amsterdam called De Pijp. I told him I came from Gein and we chatted about our friends and about what we had done. We felt there was a kind of connection between us.

During the evening an officer walked along the corridor. He opened my hatch and said, "Kotadiny, we don't normally do this, but we'll make an exception because you have such good parents. They brought you some Moluccan cake and drink from your grandmother's party." He slipped a few bowls and trays through the hatch. I could not believe my eyes! I quickly asked, "Could you please give something to my mate, Achmed, too?"

He did so. The hatch of Achmed's door was opened and his broad smile emerged.

"Thanks, Joshua!" he said. "Finally some decent food instead of that hospital stuff they are giving us here. What kind of cake is this?"

"Roti kukus from my grandmother: real Moluccan cake, dude!" I replied. We each enjoyed the dessert in our own cell and I felt a little less lonely.

The next day I had to appear in court, so I wanted to be well rested. But that night I did not sleep well. Time and again I heard boys who had just been put in a cell swearing at the police. At one point I recognized one of the voices.

"Jerry?" I shouted.

And he shouted back, "Yes?"

"It's Joshua!" I called. Jerry started to scream even louder, calling the police officers every dirty name he could think of. It was a long and restless night.

When I woke the next morning, I got some clean clothes which my mother had brought in. I put them on, had a wash, and after breakfast I was taken in handcuffs to a police car. The officers were quite friendly and asked me what I had done. I could imagine they had kids of their own, but every day at work they had to lock up boys like me. Maybe they were hoping that I had stolen some candy or had committed another small offense. The days in the cell had made me milder towards the police.

I remember the weather was nice as we drove to the court. The sun, which I had not seen for days, was shining brightly. I thought about seeing my parents again and about my friends on the street as well. I was looking forward to having a meal at McDonald's. My world had been so small for these last few days.

When we arrived at the court, a large white building full of busy people, I expected to be taken directly to the courtroom. Instead, I was escorted to a small room which looked like a cell. It was about four square meters in size and had a toilet bowl, a wooden bench, and an iron door with a hatch. There was also a button on the wall, which you could press if you needed something. Two men were sitting there already. They were constantly smoking and speaking to each other in Arabic. I asked them for a cigarette (which they gave me), but I was on my guard. I wasn't so keen on Arabs and they could easily have harmed me, because they were together and I was on my own. Luckily, nothing happened.

After a while – it seemed like hours – I was finally picked up by two guards. They took me to another room, where a young woman in a long black dress was waiting for me. She introduced herself to me as the prosecutor. I expected her to be friendly and to give me some explanation before the session started, but I was disappointed. She turned out to be the one who wanted me in jail. She pointed out to me that what I had done was against the law, Article such and such, and that she would require a jail sentence. I was shocked and impressed, and I felt very small. After this encounter I was led into the courtroom. It was a small room full of chairs. At the front there was a kind of desk, with three people sitting behind it. They were all wearing long gowns. The prosecutor I had just met was sitting on the left, the judge in the middle, and the registrar on the right. To my horror I discovered that the victim was present as well. I could see the bruises on his face. He did not look at me. I knew that I should feel something, some sense of guilt or regret, but I didn't. I was still full of anger.

Then I saw my parents in the room. In the eyes of my mother I saw sadness and despair, and suddenly I started to feel something. I found it terrible that they had to see their son in this place, in this way. They hadn't seen me for a week and now we had to meet each other here, in a courtroom. Now I was in the hands of justice and there was nothing my parents could do for me.

I took a seat on the chair which was reserved for me. My attorney was sitting next to me. That morning I had spoken with him briefly, and I knew he would defend me. The juvenile court judge was a short, skinny Dutch lady. She was a bit older and wore a pair of glasses on the tip of her nose. The victim's lawyer got permission to speak. He read out a doctor's statement, saying that the victim was suffering memory loss owing to the beating and kicking of his head and body. I felt terribly embarrassed. For a moment, I turned my head and looked back, right into my parents' eyes. I saw the disappointment, the sadness, and the fear of the sentence. Suddenly I couldn't control myself any longer. Tears started running down my cheeks. I didn't cry because I was sorry for what I had done to that man, but because of my parents' pain and sorrow. I bowed my head and looked at the floor.

Then the prosecutor started to speak. She pronounced three times thirty days of youth detention. I got even more uncomfortable. Ninety Days!

The judge noticed that my parents were in the courtroom and that they were very sad. A teacher from the school I was attending had written a letter to the court, which they read out loud during the session. He stated that he would personally keep an eye on me if I were to be released. I was surprised and touched that this teacher had done this. It made me feel accepted by people, regardless of what had happened, and that at least someone still believed in me.

The judge gave me a stern look and said, "Young man, I hope you realize that you have done something very bad. For this kind of offense you would normally get a few months' youth detention. But because you have so many good people around you and such great parents, I will charge you with violent robbery only, with thirty days of house arrest, forty hours of penal labor and a one-year conditional celestial penalty.

So, for the next thirty days you will have to go straight home from school. The justice system will keep an eye on you; you may get unexpected home visits any time."

I was relieved, thinking only about how to get back on the street as soon as possible. My parents hugged me lovingly and took me home. In the following weeks they did all they could to make sure that I could no longer get in touch with my friends. They took me to their church meetings. If I had to go to school in the morning, my dad would drive me to the nearest subway station, so I would not travel with my friends from Gein. He was hoping that I would go straight to school, but that wasn't my plan. I got off the subway at Wibautstraat, where my friends and many other boys were hanging out, dealing and stealing. Of course I made sure that I always came home at the right time, so my parents and the court officials thought that I was sticking nicely to the rules. Fortunately, this month soon went by. I wasn't yet tired of my rebellious lifestyle, so I just kept going in the same way.

42 • Finding Grace in the Gutter

8 SUMMER OF 1994

One evening when I was fifteen years old, I pretended I was going to bed early. I wished my parents goodnight and went up to my room. There I waited for the whistle of my mates, JB and MC, the sign that I was to come out.

We went first to our favorite coffee shop at the Nieuwmarkt. That's where we met every day after school, or during school time if we were skipping class. We smoked weed till we couldn't see straight anymore, played table football, and listened to reggae music. We often got so stoned that we could no longer walk properly. That evening we started at the coffee shop too. When we were stoned and drunk enough, we went to "Escape," a club near Rembrandtplein. With the whole group we danced to all the musical styles that were being played. That evening there was a group of good-looking girls. So far I had never paid much attention to girls, but I wanted to impress my friends. The alcohol and weed had wiped out any shyness or reserve about approaching these lovely ladies. I saw my friends watching me as I walked over to one of the most beautiful of them, grabbed her hand, and asked her to dance with me. A slow song by Keith Sweat, a well-known soul artist, was playing. The girl was light-colored and slim, with long curly hair. She had everything a boy could want and she said yes! This was the first time I had come so close to a girl. I had had no real relationships, because I was too young for that, but I didn't consider myself too young for sex.

It was part of our daily life: smoking, blowing, stealing, robbing, and lots of girls. Just like us boys, most of these girls got little or no attention from their father, and were therefore seeking attention from others, from boys like me and my friends

At the nearby shopping center, many youths were hanging out by the famous basketball court. Often there were dozens of young people, most of whom were wearing Nike Air Max shoes, Australian training suits, or Hazenberg sweaters, and a baseball cap on their head. The majority had one or more "King chains" around their neck, thick gold or silver chains with big, shiny links. Loud hip-hop music was blasting from the cars, which some of them had brought along: Snoop Doggy Dogg, 2Pac, and The Notorious BIG. Several boys were playing street football in the square.

At the corner of the square was a supermarket. That's where we always went as a group to get alcohol. Of course, we never paid for it. When the security guys and the manager told us off and said they would call the police, we immediately made it clear to them that they'd better not try that. We were a big group and we looked frightening; we knew that very well. We told them that we wouldn't have a problem taking revenge if they called the police. It worked: From then on we went regularly into that supermarket and took bottles of alcohol, without them saying anything.

One day, however, one of the supermarket employees got fed up with this. When Merrel went in to stock up on our supplies, he got thrown out by this employee. We were waiting to see what Merrel would do. Doing nothing wasn't an option; the supermarket employee had insulted him to the core. If he didn't take any action, he would lose his reputation within the group.

We were all drunk. One of the boys had a dagger with him. He gave it to Merrel, who ran back into the supermarket, grabbed hold of the man, and pushed the dagger into him, straight towards his heart. The young man collapsed and remained lying on the floor, in a puddle of blood. Everybody ran away, but in no time the police were on the spot. Merrel got arrested and sentenced to several months' youth detention in Groningen.

I went home, quieter than usual. Normally I didn't think much about what I was doing, but now I realized what could happen when you were intoxicated with alcohol, or drugs, or both. Merrel had gone totally wild and had lost all sense of morality. However, this could easily have happened to me as well.

Strangely enough, this realization did not make me repent. Instead, I got even harder, just like my friends. We were all aged between fourteen and seventeen, but you could not call our behavior "teenage" anymore. From the moment Merrel went to jail, our lifestyle became even more criminal. We no longer went to school but messed around with the girls in our neighborhood. In Lewi's garage we had a hangout, which we called "The underground." There we listened to hip hop, sprayed graffiti on the walls, smoked dope, and had sex with the girls we had invited to come. After we had done, blown, and drunk enough, we went downtown, carrying a ghetto blaster with hardcore rap and "bubbling music."

In the summer of 1994 we held our first house party. We as G4-Boys got loads of booze and weed, we invited all the boys from the neighborhood, and we made sure there were plenty of girls too. Ponky was good at drawing, so he made a kind of flyer as an invitation.

Actually, I was no longer allowed to go out late in the evening. So I said good night to my parents and went upstairs. There I put on music, because that's what I always did when I went to sleep. But instead of going to sleep, I put my pillows under my blankets, so it looked like I was lying in my bed. Then I stepped out my window onto the flat roof of the bike shed and from there I jumped down to the ground so I could go to my friends. One time I made too much noise. I was standing on the roof when I suddenly heard my mother's voice: "Joshua, what are you doing there?" Startled, I turned around and saw my mother sticking her head out of my bedroom window. My mind was racing.

"I lost my slippers; maybe they are here!"

My mother told me to come in. "Are you crazy, standing on the roof at half past one at night? Next time I'll tell your father!" she said.

"It won't happen again, Mom," I answered politely. But a few minutes later I was on the roof again. This time I made sure there was no sound, and soon I was on my way to the party, which was being held at a friend's house. When I arrived and glanced through the window, I saw everybody blowing, dancing, and drinking alcohol. I opened the door and was almost knocked over by Lewi, who was sick because he had drunk too much.

Soon I was fully immersed in the party atmosphere. With a joint in one hand and a beer in the other I felt I could take on the whole world. So, when I heard my mate Kisri say that his neighbor, Matthijs, had gone on holiday, I immediately came up with a great plan. Matthijs had a moped, a Gilera, which we thought was amazing. If you had a Gilera, you were really cool. But Matthijs was a Dutch boy and I couldn't stand him. I had fallen out with him a few times already and, sure enough, I had taken revenge several times. His room was on the street side of the house, so when his window was open I had slipped in a few times and stolen all his expensive Australian training suits. This time, however, we wanted to go even further: MC, Kisri, and I would break into his garage and take the Gilera. That would teach him a lesson.

Kisri took a pair of leather gloves, a breaker, and some more tools we could use to break into the garage and to start the Gilera. I took a few more puffs on my joint and the three of us went outside to Matthijs' house. When we arrived at the garage we tried to open the door with the jimmy, but it was harder than we had expected. We had a go with all the tools but nothing really worked. Eventually we got frustrated and started kicking and banging on the door, but the garage remained firmly shut. It was too well protected.

Seriously disappointed, we went back to the party. We drowned our misery in alcohol and then got distracted by the girls. Later that night Lewi, Ponky, and I got so drunk that we passed out in the front yard. As soon as I started to sober up, I went home. (I had to sleep somewhere, after all.) As always, I felt uncomfortable as I was walking home. Not only was I afraid of getting caught being out at night, I also felt guilty towards God and my parents. They did their best to look after me, but the street was drawing me and pulling me away. Coming home, I would often see my mother on her knees in her little room. I knew she was praying for me. It touched me, but not enough to change my life. The attraction of street life was still too strong for me.

9 FROM BAD TO WORSE

On another evening I had escaped through the window again and gone off with my friends. We had been roaming the inner city in a large group. When we got fed up with this we took the night bus home. In our opinion the bus was taking too long to leave, so we started messing about. We grew so wild that one of the passengers got up and told us to calm down. It seemed to work a bit, but the man was not satisfied. He kept talking to us and told me that I probably didn't get enough attention from my mother, and that I was causing havoc on the night bus because of that. He shouldn't have mentioned my mother.

A red haze descended before my eyes and I stormed at him. Strangely enough, he came towards me at the same time. I punched him right in the stomach and from all sides my friends came to my aid. They started kicking and beating him. My friend MC kept kicking his head until my other friends pulled him away. The man staggered to his feet, with blood running down his face. He looked horrible.

Soon we heard the sirens of several police cars approaching. The bus driver had closed the doors, so we could not get out. It suddenly dawned on me that I still had a one-year conditional celestial penalty. That made it even more necessary to escape. I spotted a sliding roof above me, which was easy to open. MC and I quickly climbed onto the roof and jumped off the bus. While running away we took off our jackets and hats so that the police would not recognize us on the basis of the description the bus driver would undoubtedly give them.

That time we didn't get caught. But we became increasingly restless and violent.

Every night we went downtown, coffee shop in, coffee shop out. We didn't have a clue what we were doing. We often brought our ghetto blaster along and played gangster rap or bubbling music. One evening we were on the platform of the subway station, on our way to town. We were with a group of ten boys and we were making a lot of noise. A metro driver got out, came over to us, and pushed one of my friends over. We could not let that happen.

The ten of us stormed towards him and started beating him up. From all directions conductors and metro drivers came running to help their colleague. It turned into a huge fight. I flung myself at one of the metro drivers with a flying kick, which hit him hard in his upper body. However, instead of shrinking back, he quickly pulled a blackjack out of his pocket and began to strike me. He kept hitting my arms and legs, but I didn't retreat. The harder the blows, the more I kicked and hit back. Finally MC stopped me, saying, "You're crazy, Josh! Let's go! 0-5 is coming and when that blackjack hits your head, you're dead!" I realized he was right. But when I turned to run away, I saw that there were dozens of people standing around us. To my great horror there were several people I knew among them. I did not have much time to think about that, though, because the whole group was running up the escalator. At the same time, dozens of officers came running down the escalator. It was weird: The policemen were so focussed on getting to the fight that they did not notice us on the escalator, fleeing from the station.

Cracking up with laughter, we ran into the inner city. Those stupid police had run right past their targets, without even recognizing us!

9. From bad to worse

Not only did we fight with passersby and subway employees, but also with other youth gangs. On Friday nights there were bubbling parties in the neighborhood, which were attended by all kinds of groups from the Bijlmer area. Besides us there were boys from the other districts. One gang was stronger, another danced better. The gangs eyed one another suspiciously and there was always competition, in part because of the girls.

One gang we had already noticed a couple of times came from Kraaiennest district. One of their leaders was Clifton, a short guy with an aggressive appearance and one golden tooth. He always looked angry. That night our eyes met several times, and we tried to intimidate each other with our stares. As we Gein boys went to our favorite snack bar after the party, it turned out that the guys from Kraaiennest had had the same idea. In the snack bar I stood face to face with Clifton again, and this time it didn't stop at angry looks. Within no time we were engaged in a loud argument, which I soon concluded by giving him a full blow in the face and smacking his head against the snack bar's display window. From the left, right, and back I felt kicks and fist blows raining down on my body. Clifton's friends had come to help him, but I was mad with rage. I threw him onto one of the tables, while more boys joined in the fight. I searched my inner pocket for the butcher's knife I always carried with me, but then realized that I had just given it to my friend Kisri. He wasn't with us that evening.

We got kicked out of the snack bar and the fight went on outside. I picked up a brick to throw it at Clifton's head, but my cousin Bootje stopped me. He wanted to get some friends to help us, and the two of us walked off. Clifton and his friends came after us and picked up the brick I had dropped. I saw it and quickly ran away, but then I thought, "Fleeing is for wimps!" Reckless because of all the drugs and alcohol, I stopped in my tracks. Clifton threw the brick at my head and I just managed to duck and avoid it. He picked up another brick and threw again – and missed again. Clifton and I stood facing each other; I was in a frenzy. Then I felt someone grab me and pull me back. It was one of my cousin's friends. Instead of joining in the fight, the others drew us apart. At that moment I felt sorry, but afterwards I realized it was a good thing that I hadn't had my knife with me. I would definitely have stabbed Clifton. From that moment on, I made sure that I always had a knife, a gun, or some tear gas with me to protect myself. I became increasingly aggressive and violent.

There were some girls in our group as well. One evening, Priscilla and Soraya came to us and told us that some boys from another district were bothering them. One of the boys was called Ronny. We wanted to defend our girls and went to look for these boys to teach them a lesson. When we found their hangout, Bootje and Kisri hid around the corner. I planned to call Ronny to "have a chat" and then Bootje and Kisri would beat the hell out of him.

The plan worked. As soon as I called to Ronny, he came out of the garden. At the same time, Bootje and Kisri came running around the corner and Bootje punched him hard in the face: CRACK! Ronny screamed like a pig. He ran away and we followed, kicking him and shouting, "Don't you ever touch our chicks again!" We dragged him to the next street corner, where two other friends stood waiting for us. We all jumped on him, kicking and beating him as hard as we could. Ronny squealed in pain, but his friends were nowhere to be seen.

Eventually he was down on all fours on the street. I stood in front of him and gave him a final kick, right in the face. Then four men came running towards us with huge baseball bats.

"Niggers! Dirty niggers!" they shouted. We ran off in all directions. These grown-ups with bats were a number too big for us.

A few weeks later, we all received a letter from the police: We had to appear in court. I was lucky: Bootje and Kisri had said that I was there but had not kicked anyone. For a while Ronny was walking around with a broken nose and broken ribs, and whenever he saw us he and his gang made sure they kept at a safe distance. He never bothered us again.

As G-Boys, we loved not only drink, drugs, and girls, but also football. Some of us could have been professional footballers if we had not chosen street life. Of course, we were all Ajax supporters. When Ajax won the Champions League in 1995, there was a big party. With the whole group we celebrated this event with loads of alcohol and weed.

When I got home, we had visitors. I stuck my head around the corner and my father asked me what I was up to. This was my chance! I said I had forgotten something and that I was just going to get it. I would be back within an hour. Because we had visitors, my dad left it and I ran off to the subway station.

All my mates were already there. When we heard that Ajax's F-side (the hard core supporters) were at Leidseplein, we went there too. The subway was full of Ajax hooligans; we were partying all the way from Gein to Waterlooplein. We sang Ajax songs, drank cans of beer, and scanned the name of the top scorer, Patrick Kluivert. I forgot the time.

With the whole group we went to Leidseplein, which was packed with Ajax supporters. It was by now one o'clock in the morning, but everybody was still full-on singing and chanting. Some guys jumped on the roofs of flower stalls and on top of the bus shelters and began to smash them. But then one of my friends called, "Riot cops!" The riot police were coming. We heard sirens and police horses galloping around the square. Soon there were two camps: hundreds of Ajax supporters opposite the heavily armed police force. We threw bricks, cans, and beer bottles at the officers. In our drunken frenzy we wanted to destroy everything and everyone. The police guys tried to drive us back, but we were unstoppable. Suddenly I heard: "Bang! Bang! Bang! "The cops had started shooting and we ran away. The ME shot with bullets which, when they hit you, released a gas which caused a burning sensation on your skin. Ponky got hit. He was trying to cool down in a puddle of rainwater on the street. MC and I tried to help him, but a few cops came running towards us. Ponky was completely out of his mind. He and some other Ajax supporters ran straight towards the police officers and started beating them with whatever they could get their hands on. MC also picked up a stick and ran into the fray.

The police guys kept on shooting and hitting us with rubber bats and we ran away, but soon we turned around to attack again. It was like a war. There was screaming, beating, kicking, and shooting all around us. Hundreds of Ajax supporters were busy breaking down bus stops, shelters, and shop windows. Shops were looted; police officers got beaten up.

Eventually we pulled out and started heading into town to continue the celebration in the clubs and cafés. It was five o'clock in the morning when I finally went home. As I opened the door of our living room I saw my father sitting on the couch. He was furious.

My dad got up and told me to sit down. His eyes were flashing with anger – rightly so. I obeyed; I had no idea what he wanted. Then I saw him pull out his belt. He struck hard – right beside me on the couch. Then on the other side, and again, and again. Sometimes he hit my hand or my arm, but it was never his intention to really hurt me. Despite his anger, he still had enough self-control and love for me not to beat me till I bled. I bowed my head. I had done more than enough to deserve this beating.

But my life did not change.

10 MONEY

In order to buy weed and alcohol, I needed money. Lots of money. So far, I had mainly got it by stealing from my father's wallet or by burglary and robbery. But at my new school I learned a better way to get money.

I was expelled from school several times, but I was still of an age for compulsory education. Eventually I was placed in job training, for which I had to work at a toy store a few days a week and attend class one day a week. Most boys in my class were involved in crime; they were from a Surinamese or Moroccan background and lived in West Amsterdam. They walked around in the most expensive Nike Air Max trainers, and wore heavy gold chains and expensive branded jumpers. I wanted that too! I asked one of the guys how they got all those things. "Bustling," he said. The boy's name was Mau. He was short and stocky, with dreadlocks hanging in front of his eyes and two golden front teeth.

"How do you do that?" I asked, and he held up a bag full of little white balls filled with powder. I had no idea what it was.

"This is dope, friend," he said. "Coke. All the junkies in Amsterdam use it for basing. If you sell it for me, you'll get one-third of the money and I'll get the rest."

It did not matter how much I got; I only thought, I'll get money!

From that day I could be found everywhere with the dope: at

Central Station, on the Nieuwmarkt, in Wibautstraat. Wherever the junkies were hanging out, I was there to sell stuff.

Things went well, especially when I also started working for JB. He had approached me when I was hanging out in the mall with the G-Boys. He said, "Josh, I know you're selling. I also have good stuff! Standing around all day long, drinking and smoking and fighting, won't get you anywhere. Selling lai will get you far, bro!"

I could tell by his looks that JB had come far: He was wearing the latest pattas, he was the first to have a mobile phone, and he had a nice leather jacket. And he and his brother were the first of our group to drive a BMW 5. I also wanted that, and asked him, "What do you have, bro?"

He gave me a mysterious smile and said, "This is not dope or Buddha; this is the real deal at house parties! It's XTC! Flying pigeons!"

JB had a proposal: "All you have to do is resell. You get a quarter of the proceeds and I get the rest. If I see you're getting the hang of it, you'll be given more doekoe." I agreed, and that's how I stumbled into the world of drug dealing. I started as a runner and wanted to be known as a dealer. I started taking the XTC pills to house parties throughout the whole neighborhood. It brought me a lot of money, but also a lot of stress. Sometimes someone else sold the pills for me, but then I had to wait and see whether I would get my money. On one occasion, things were taking too long for me. I had a sharp knife in my pocket to put the other guy down, in case he came up with a story that he had got robbed or lost the money. I still remember how I felt. We were sitting next to each other at the bar and I was determined to put him down on the spot. But he picked up a stack of money and gave me my share. Just as well, because I still had to pay Tjogga.

JB lived just outside Amsterdam. After buying some weed with my share of the money, I took a train to his house. We smoked the weed together and then he said, "Soon I'll be off to Suriname, but I will leave my stuff with one of my sources."

That was the last time I saw JB. Later, I heard that he had got jailed for years for murder. During a fight he had stabbed someone in the neck.

From one of my friends I heard that one of the tattas in the neighborhood had a 9mm gun. I was quite interested. I made an appointment with this guy to buy his gun for a few hundred guilders. We agreed to meet somewhere on the outskirts of our district and I asked him to show me the gun. Both of us had brought some friends along. The boy pulled out the gun, loaded it, and gave it to me. I did not intend to buy it, but he didn't know that. I carefully examined the gun, then calmly pointed it at his head and said, "Now it's mine! Turn around and get out of my face. If you look around, you're dead!" The boys around us were all shocked by my action. But the guy saw in my eyes that I meant what I said, so he turned around and left.

I still belonged to the group of young G-Boys. We took the group of older boys from Gein, who were all big gangsters, as our examples. When they were walking around the mall, we often "accidentally" cycled past them on our stolen bikes. Just after I had won the gun, we cycled past them again. One of the guys called me over. His name was Joernie. He was aAntillean and we knew he was a top gangster. He had heard what I had done and he liked the fact that I had the guts to do this. That's why he asked me and my mate Merrel, who by now had finished his sentence for the stabbing, whether we wanted to work for him.

We had to swallow little balls of dope and fly to Suriname. We would earn a lot of money.

We met in the mall a couple of times to talk about it. I was interested; it sounded easy and I was keen to earn a few thousand guilders. I did not think of the danger. I just didn't know how to explain to my parents that I would be away for a week.

But after a few conversations with Joernie, the story ended. One night, I heard from my friends that Joernie had been hit by a bullet from his own gun. He was running from the police and had his loaded gun in his pocket. As he ran the gun fell out and went off and the bullet pierced his stomach. Joernie didn't survive.

I was deeply impressed because it was the first time that someone I knew had died in this way. I felt gutted as well that the Suriname adventure wasn't now going to happen. In retrospect, I see it as God's protection; if I had smuggled drugs into Suriname, I would certainly have been caught.

In the meantime, my relationship with Mau had improved. I ran grams of coke for him; I wanted to continue and work my way up in the scene. Mau and I built up some kind of friendship. He trusted me with his dope. One day he gave me a bag of little balls. I forgot to count them, so when I got home I looked for a safe place to do that. I sat down on the toilet, but I was so focussed on my dope that I forgot to lock the door. When I had taken the coke balls out of the bag and was about to count them, the toilet door suddenly opened. It was my father.

He looked at me, he looked at the coke, and then he slammed the toilet door shut. I felt the pain I saw in his eyes. The sadness and disappointment: He had left his own past of drug addiction, and now he found his own son doing this. I stayed in the toilet for a couple of minutes. But then I took a deep breath and stood up. I had to face the consequences; this was my own fault. I went out of the toilet and walked to my father, who was in the living room. He pulled the bag out of my hands and said, "Give me that rubbish! Stay here on the couch. I'll be back."

I just did what my dad said, because I saw that this time there was no way out. I felt caught but also guilty. I was ashamed of myself.

My father took the bag in his hand and walked to the toilet. I thought he needed to wee, but then I heard him flush the toilet eight or ten times. I stood up, walked over to him, and saw that he was flushing all the dope down the toilet!

My guilt and shame were replaced by anger and fear. Mau! If he finds out what happened to this dope, I'll be in big trouble! With a quivering voice I said to my father, "Dad, what are you doing?" But he didn't say a word and kept flushing away the dope. I walked back to the living room, almost crying with despair. I would get into serious trouble on the street! However, I did not want to tell my parents that. I was ashamed to tell them the truth, and I also afraid that my dad would do whatever he could to keep me away from my friends.

So when my father asked me with a desperate look in his eyes how I had gotten that dope, I lied with a trembling voice, telling him that I had found it between some subway benches. In the Amsterdam subway, junkies were using coke all the time, and when the police came they'd often throw their stuff away. My father knew this, but I saw doubt flickering across his face. He was hoping that I was telling the truth. We didn't talk about it again.

11 THE SUMMER CAMP

From that moment on, I tried to take things easy. My life mainly rotated around trying to evade Mau. I didn't dare tell him what had happened to the dope, but I still owed him a few hundred bucks. I didn't have the money. So I just stopped contacting him, and at every party where I was likely to meet him I tried to avoid him. But on the street I heard that Mau was looking for me. He sensed that something was dodgy. Mau was sixteen years old and owned a revolver, a Colt 35. He wouldn't shrink from shooting me if I didn't show up with the money.

One evening, I didn't manage to avoid him. I met him at a party and he asked why he had hadn't heard anything from me. I tried to beat around the bush, but he became increasingly aggressive and began to threaten me. That's why I told him I'd get the money right away. I disappeared and did not return to the party.

I had always thought that Amsterdam was a big city, but now I knew Mau was looking for me, it seemed like a small village. I met him in the strangest places, where I had never seen him before. If I could not escape, I made up an excuse and said I would get the money right away, but I did not get back to him. At every party and every hangout I went to, I felt uneasy. I was constantly afraid of running into Mau. Fortunately, we didn't go to the same school.

I told my friends that I had to pay Mau back but didn't have the money. At one point I heard from them that Mau was tired of waiting. The next time he would not talk anymore, but act. I knew what kind of guy he was, so I got really nervous. I considered myself too young to die. However, on the street I did not want to show how scared I was, so I walked around with all the weapons I might possibly need.

On a hot summer day I came home after smoking and drinking with some friends on the street. At home, I met my brother, Emiliano, who was cleaning. As he was vacuuming he asked me spontaneously, "Josh, in two weeks' time we'll be going on a camp with the youth of the Victory Outreach Church. Do you want to come with us?" I asked him where it was and for how long, and he told me that they would be going to Limburg for five days.

Of course, this meant nothing to me, but the idea of having a five-day break from the fear of Mau and of being able to hide in Limburg appealed to me. So, to Emiliano's great astonishment, I said yes.

The evening before we left for the camp we had another family party. I got so drunk that I got into an argument with some of my relatives. My sister, aunts, and my grandmother intervened and told me off for misbehaving. I felt humiliated and walked away in anger. As I kicked the door open to go outside, some uncles came after me to calm me down and talk to me. At that moment, I heard someone calling out, "Hey, where's my money?" I turned around and saw Mau and his mates cycling towards me.

Suddenly everything came together: I was having a row with my family, I was being pushed around by a bunch of women, and now the dealers were coming to get me. There I stood face to face with Mau and his mates, with no way of escape.

To my surprise, my brother, Emiliano, suddenly came running towards us. He was always calm, but now he shouted at Mau, "What do you want? Do you want to fight?" I was flabbergasted. I had expected Emiliano to be intimidated by Mau and his friends, but it was the other way around. Mau said, "Okay, you're lucky, Josh! I'm leaving now, but wo meet ekandra!" And off he went with his friends.

I didn't yet realize what was happening, but suddenly it all became too much for me. My mother's youngest brother came over to me and said, "I'll bring you home." I fell into his arms and began to cry. I felt anger, incomprehension, pain, despair, and disappointment in myself, all at the same time. My uncle held me and comforted me. Then he took me home.

The next day I had to be at the Victory Outreach Church in time for the service which was to be held before we left for the summer camp. I saw dozens of young people with bags and suitcases. It was my parents' church, but I hardly ever went there so most of the young people did not know me.

I was standing on the fringes, looking a bit lost, when a sturdy, dark young man walked towards me. He said, "You are Joshua, right? Your life is going to change! I'm going to work with you during the camp. My name is David and I was also a criminal, but Jesus changed my life." He turned out to be one of the youth leaders and he probably wanted to encourage me, but his efforts had rather the opposite effect: I did not want to go anymore! I had no idea what to expect, but I also realized there was no way out.

During the bus trip everyone was sitting next to a friend. I preferred to be alone because I did not want to mix with these crazy Christians. The campsite was situated in a beautiful wooded hilly area in Limburg. We got out of the bus and were immediately approached by one of the youth leaders.

This tall young man was called Regillio. He welcomed us and told us the rules straight away. The one that impressed me most was: Smoking is not allowed during the camp. Anyone who smokes will be sent back by train to Amsterdam.

I had a packet of cigarettes in my pocket. I tried to hide it by putting my hand on my pocket. I did not want to lose my cigarettes, but I certainly did not want to go home! I was relaxing for a few days without constantly having to look over my shoulder to make sure Mau wasn't around.

Fortunately, there were a few other boys who had only come to the camp for fun. One of them was Rangelo. He was five years older than me and was also known in East Amsterdam because of his criminal behavior. He wanted to break with his old life, but he did not have enough discipline to hand in his cigarettes. In addition, there was a nice Surinamese girl who also smoked. Almost every day we secretly met up to smoke cigarettes and talk about all sorts of things.

On one of those evenings Rangelo and I agreed to have a smoke on the fire escape. I still had some cigarettes, so Rangelo got one from me. After smoking my stub, I went back inside, where some others were playing cards. Rangelo was still smoking when Regillio, the youth leader, came by. Busted!

"Hand me those cigarettes now!" the strict youth leader commanded. I gave Rangelo a desperate look. Rangelo understood me and said, "Sorry, I can't give them to you, because they're not mine!"

"Whose are they?" Regillio asked. I started sweating; if Rangelo said they were mine, I would be sent home. And I did not want that! To my surprise, I got on really well with the young people who were there. Most of them were about my age, but they were very different from me. They were friendly and relaxed and they did not need weed, alcohol, or other means to be happy. I hadn't expected that I would feel at home so soon. Fortunately, Rangelo went on to say he did not want to tell who he had got the cigarettes from. He had to hand them in, but didn't have to go home. And neither did I, to my relief. These young people were real: I didn't have to pretend; I could just be who I was. After a few days it seemed like I had been in the group for years. I felt so at home that I had forgotten where I came from.

One evening we had to create and act out a short drama performance as a group. I joined in enthusiastically and really enjoyed it. I was also allowed to play drums while my brother and others were rapping. My cousin, who was a good drummer, had taught me some rhythms, and I was able to use those well during the camp. The camp's music director, Raoel, welcomed me into his band. He was excited about my drum skills and I was asked to play more often. However, my repertoire was limited to hip hop and reggae, so that's what they got with each church song. Raoel and I became good friends.

During the meals, the youngsters took turns praying out loud. That fascinated me. Not because prayer in itself was new to me – my parents prayed every day. However, I was always surprised when I saw young people pray. Whether they were praying for dinner, for each other, or for something else, I was always impressed. I wondered where these young people got all those words from, to come up with such beautiful prayers.

One morning, it was my turn. The youth leader said, "Okay, boys and girls, before we have breakfast, I want to ask Joshua to lead us in prayer and bless the food. Joshua, could you please stand?"

I slowly got up, holding my hat in front of my eyes. It was quiet in the hall, despite there being about thirty young people present. It felt like all eyes were fixed on me. I was sure that all the young people were wondering: How is this Joshua going to pray?

I took a deep breath and said, "Lord God, thank you for this morning; thank you for this day. I thank you that I can come to you with all my cares. Bless this breakfast, amen." I slowly opened my eyes and suddenly all the youngsters started applauding. I could tell by their ovation that they were very glad that I had tried, and that I was praying sincerely.

I felt safe and loved in this group, but I was also aware of the contrast with the group I had been part of over the last few years. These young people had a very different mind-set than that group. They looked the same and wore the same clothes, but my new friends didn't need drugs and alcohol to feel good. That attracted me, but I did not know how to become like that myself.

For the last evening a young preacher had been invited. We started with singing, prayer, and dancing. It was so much fun! Then the preacher came forward. His talk was appealing and powerful. Some of the things he said went straight to my heart. He told us that Jesus can help you if you are in trouble. Well, I was definitely in trouble! The next day I would return to Amsterdam, and my life would be in danger. He also told us that Jesus is love. That struck a sensitive chord. Love was the very thing I had always missed most and had been so desperately searching for.

The young pastor told the gospel in a very simple way, but it was exactly what I needed. After his message, he called those who wanted prayer to come forward. Many young people went forward and gave their lives to Jesus while they were crying and praying. I stayed were I was. I was trying hard to think soberly: This was just emotion; it didn't mean anything. However, at the same time I felt deep in my heart that this was the moment to make a decision: Would I stay where I was, in my miserable life of drugs, alcohol, and crime? Or would I take the step into a new life, a life like the one I had come to know during the past few days? A life with God?

A fierce battle raged in my heart until I couldn't contain it any longer. I stood up, walked forward, and began to cry like a little child. Immediately, some youth leaders came over to me. They laid hands on me and began to pray with me. I kept crying; I didn't care who saw me. I was so full of pain and regret about everything I had done in the past.

The youth leader embraced me and led me in a prayer of repentance. As I prayed with him, I accepted Jesus into my life. Then I felt freedom flowing through me. It was as if a heavy burden had been lifted. I had never felt so good!

After the meeting I went back to the dormitory room which I shared with some other boys. Two of my roommates, with whom I had been smoking over the last few days and mocking the strict leadership, hadn't gone to the meeting. When I came in, they asked, "And was it boring?" I still wanted to look cool, so I said, "Yeah, very boring!" I tried to feel the anger we had shared over the past few days, but it didn't work. I realized that Jesus really had set me free, even from that anger.

From that day on everything changed. I started spending more time with Christian young people and quickly established close friendships with some boys from the church, among whom were Raoel, Regillio, and David. Every Sunday I went to church. I sought distraction in the various activities that were being organized. At the same time, my bond with my brother was getting closer. Together with him I set up a gospel band, for which I became the drummer. Meanwhile my sister had come home again. She was pregnant and had a daughter, Alvah. This child also brought our family closer together. My sister went to church more and more and it seemed that everything in our family was slowly beginning to recover.

My life had changed completely. My parents were happy and relieved and told me that I had made the best possible choice. Instead of going to the coffee shops, I now went to youth services. I made new, Christian, friends. Meanwhile, I tried to avoid my old friends as much as possible. If I encountered them, I told them about my experience with God. They were very impressed, but still felt too attracted to their lives on the street to make the same choice.

In the new school year I began on a new working–learning program. I wanted to make a fresh start in my life and was determined not to waste this opportunity. The first few weeks went well. I teamed up with those boys in my class who also wanted to learn and I tried to avoid the others who were mainly smoking, playing cards, and chilling in the aula. I enjoyed going to school. In the breaks there were often "rap battles": A group of boys would stand in a circle and anyone who wanted to could jump into the middle of the circle to show off his rap skills. I liked to join in as I had become a good rapper during my time on the street. I also got good grades, so I thought I was doing fine.

Until, one day after school, I saw a group of boys standing in a corner. From a distance, I could smell a strong odor of weed. I was walking between my new friends, but one of the boys who were smoking called to me and said, "Do you want to smoke? We have enough!" To my surprise I immediately responded: I walked over to them and took a puff. It was months since I had smoked, so it felt uncomfortable, but oh, how good it was! The feeling of guilt soon disappeared.

From that moment on I led a kind of double life. On the one hand, I had my church friends, I enjoyed the youth activities of the church, and I wanted to follow Jesus. On the other hand, I could not completely let go of the weed and the alcohol. Occasionally I also saw my old friends, even though a lot had changed for them too. Some were in jail for armed robbery or smuggling drugs; others had become real junkies, whom I would see lurching drunk across the street at eight o'clock in the morning. I wasn't jealous of them or fully one of them, but I didn't manage to pull out completely either. The church offered only minimal guidance. I felt left on my own and unable to cut all the connections completely. Nevertheless, deep in my heart I knew that I wanted to serve Jesus. He was the One who gave me real peace inside.

12 MIRJAM

One day my father said it was time for us to go to another church, which would be better for our family. I found it hard to leave my friends from the youth group, but at the same time I was looking forward to making a fresh start in a new congregation.

The first time I went to our new church was for a youth evening. Together with my brother I went to a church in Slotervaart, where dozens of young people were present. There were various performances of singing, rap, and dance. I was sitting in the back when a group of nice girls appeared on stage and started a drama/mime performance. They were all between sixteen and twenty years old and, of course, I was interested in them. A pretty, dark girl with braids and an attractive appearance struck me the most, especially because of her smile.

I asked the boy next to me what kind of group this was and what the girl's name was. Actually, I was only interested in that one girl, but of course I tried to conceal it. That one special girl turned out to be Mirjam, and I immediately got a warning: She was popular with the boys but "hard to get." She loved God very much, liked studying, and was a very smart girl, so it wouldn't be easy to get her.

When the group performed a song later in the evening, I

could not keep my eyes off Mirjam again. Inside of me, I felt a strange kind of joy bubbling up, and deep within I heard a voice saying, "She's going to be your wife." When the evening was over, my brother was excited about the whole event, but I was just full of that girl I had seen. Yet I hadn't even spoken to her!

On Sunday, we went to our new church as a family. It didn't take long for me to connect with the young people; I had learned how to do that on the street. They seemed as nice to me as the youth from our previous church. Here they also made music and, young as they were, they were really dedicated to God. That also motivated me to serve God. During the service Mirjam was on stage again to sing. I couldn't focus on the songs; I just kept looking at her.

Soon I became friends with Howard, a boy from our new church. His mother had raised four children on her own, as his father did not live at home anymore. We got on really well and also met up outside of church. I told Howard about my life on the street and what Jesus had done in my life, and he was hugely impressed.

I was still captivated by Mirjam and Howard had an eye on Shilly, Mirjam's friend. We talked a lot about them, and Howard told me that I would have to make a great effort to get Mirjam's attention. She was smart and beautiful and wanted a guy who had his life in order and knew what he wanted. I still hadn't plucked up enough courage to speak to Mirjam. According to Howard, I should proceed with a great deal of patience, and first try to build up a friendship. He knew a good occasion when I could meet her: Every year she attended a conference where hundreds of Christians from across Europe came together. We decided to go there too to try to speak to Mirjam. For three days we went to the conference and every now and then we caught a glimpse of the beautiful Mirjam, but I did not succeed in establishing contact with her. Still, I did not give up, and eventually I even managed to persuade her to give me her phone number. I called her up and we had a pleasant conversation. After that we chatted regularly during and after youth evenings. I did my best to make a good impression on her and carefully revealed to her that I wanted more. Her response, however, was different from what I was hoping. She told me that she had different ideas for her life. She was serious about her study and wanted to focus on what God wanted. It was better to stay friends and not to expect too much.

I was deeply disappointed. I was head over heels in love with her and convinced that I would share my life with her, but, for the time being, that seemed to be completely out of the question.

At that time the church leadership wasn't able to help me with all my issues either. There were problems in the church: Several people were leaving, even some of the parents of my friends. Several young people were disconnecting from church too and starting to go to clubs or coffee shops.

I felt less and less at home in the church. One Sunday service and one prayer meeting a week weren't enough for me. I needed more to challenge, adjust, and reshape my life. In hindsight, I think I should have gone to a Bible college, where I would get full-time input in my life.

I was disappointed because Mirjam did not want me (yet), I found church boring, and I felt uncomfortable. I was too noisy and too wild, and felt like I had to get rid of my street manners in order to be accepted in the church. My passion for serving Jesus faded and I started thinking about going back to my old friends. At the same time I did not want that: It wouldn't be any good if I were to go back to them with my tail between my legs, after claiming for a long time that Jesus had radically changed me. Neither did I want to let go of Mirjam, as I was still in love with her and we often had long and positive conversations. She used to tell me how she saw life and how she wanted to serve God and encourage young people to make a choice for Jesus. It did not matter to me what she was talking about; I took every opportunity to be with her because she was the only one with whom I felt safe and trusted. However, she just wanted to be a good friend to me, nothing more than that.

Howard struggled with similar problems. He too was searching for his identity in Christ and his place in the church, but didn't receive adequate guidance from the church. One evening, while we were getting bored at his home, we decided to go and find a good joint. Perhaps that would make us feel better. From that moment on we did the same thing every week, and I slowly slipped back into my old life.

In the church I was drumming and rapping, I went to Bible studies and church services, but it did not really mean much to me. As a result, I became increasingly indifferent, and at times I even went to church stoned. There was little positive attention from the church leadership. Instead, I was regularly told what I wasn't doing right.

Howard and I got together more and more. We became best buddies and pulled each other further down. For example, we went joyriding one night in a car belonging to my uncle, who was staying with us temporarily. I was meeting my old friends from Gein more often, and although they asked me what I was doing and why I wasn't in church, I was back to the same old life. I started smoking with them again and going to discos. Yet it wasn't quite the same as before: The group was smaller now, as several boys were in prison and others had gotten on with their lives.

Things changed when Mirjam called me and told me that God had a plan for my life. I wouldn't want you to throw that away, she said. She sounded different from the last time we had talked to each other, and I felt hope rising again. We talked more often after this, and Mirjam told me she had thought about the two of us. After her studies, she wanted more contact with me so that we could get to know each other better.

This was the push I needed. I started enjoying going to church again, mostly to see Mirjam, but God was using this to bring me closer to Him. I started to engage actively in church again, especially in the worship band. After church on Sunday we usually talked together and went for an ice cream or a walk in the Vondelpark. One day I surprised her with a big, expensive teddy bear. I did not tell her that I had stolen it from the toy store where I had done my job training.

After a few months I plucked up all my courage and asked Mirjam if she wanted to be my girlfriend, and she said yes! It seemed like my world was reversing at that moment. I now had a good reason not to go out with my old friends anymore and to leave the coffee shops behind. I told Howard that I really wanted to serve Jesus one hundred percent because He had helped me and given me a girlfriend. Howard was very happy for me.

In the church everyone had to get used to our relationship. Mirjam had always been a faithful believer, but I had a very different background. So they kept a watchful eye on us, which felt a bit suffocating at times. However, I did my utmost to prove my good intentions and to adapt. Our parents also did their best: We came together as families and my parents and Mirjam's mother prayed together for us. My father suggested that we should go somewhere together every month, in order to keep our relationship fresh and strengthen our friendship. After all, we were still very young: seventeen and eighteen. During these outings we talked about our desires for the future. I had no idea what to expect and was living from day to day, but Mirjam knew exactly what she wanted.

When I had finished my education, I had fallen into a black hole. Mirjam was studying hard at college, but I had no idea what God wanted for my life. I tried all sorts of jobs: at a telecoms company and in the cooling department of a wholesale company; I applied for a job with the National Air Force and at a gym, but nothing worked out well. I had developed a fear of failure in the area of learning, so I didn't dare to go to school again.

Fortunately, besides God, I had Mirjam in my life. We often went out together and had a lot of fun. We tried to keep our relationship as much as possible on a friendship level, so that we would not get tempted to become too intimate. We often went for a walk, ate out, or went to the cinema, and we were so in love with each other that we knew we would be together for a long time.

13 ITALY

When we had been together for three years, Mirjam had to go abroad to do an internship as part of her studies. This meant that I had to do without her for half a year and get on with my life and my relationship with God. My father knew of a place where Mirjam could do her internship, Victory Outreach Napoli, a church in Italy that was working among addicts and homeless people. A few months later, we took Mirjam to Schiphol Airport. It was very hard for me to let her go, but I knew I had to. I knew that I really had to trust in God alone, now that the security that Mirjam gave me was temporarily removed. In the church, I did not have any other confidants; I had only found my place there thanks to Mirjam. She had been part of this church from birth.

Mirjam was usually my distraction. Now that she was away for a while, I had to spend my time in different ways. My relationship with God had been so closely connected to Mirjam, but now I had to build that relationship with God alone.

At that time, I worked in a bar on Rembrandtplein to earn some extra money. After a while, I was asked to take on night shifts. For a while I tried to behave, but in that environment there were many temptations. The music, the women, the drink... However, the money from the fees, about 100 guilders a week, came in really handy, so, instead of spending extra time with God, I threw myself into work.

After work, the bartender often offered the employees a drink. At first I managed to have the discipline to go home straight after work, but after a few weeks I felt so lonely that I accepted a Coca Cola. We chatted about all sorts of things and it was really cozy. Every night I stayed a little longer, first having soft drinks, but after a time, accepting a whisky. Soon I got used to drinking alcohol after work.

One night, I left work slightly drunk and walked past a club that was still open. The doorman, whom I knew from before, asked me to come in. I went in. At first I enjoyed it: the music, the whisky, the dancing! But as soon as I started to sober up I wanted to leave as quickly as possible. I felt the emptiness, I felt lonely, I felt like a loser. I quickly went outside and sat down in tears on a bench. I asked God for forgiveness and wisdom and to show me His plan for my life. That same week I applied for another job.

Mirjam and I called each other regularly and we also wrote letters. I could not wait to see her, but I did not tell her how much I was struggling. She was having a very good time in Italy and enjoying the work for God. She asked me to come over for a week. It would do me good, she said, and I thought it was a great idea. Soon afterwards I flew to Naples, where I could finally embrace my sweet Mirjam. I was happy but nervous at the same time because I had an important mission: I wanted to propose to Mirjam. I was well prepared: I had bought an engagement ring and a little teddy bear with a heart, in which I could hide the ring. It would happen during my last evening in Naples.

We had a wonderful week together. We enjoyed Italy and each other's company. I also helped in the church evangelization program among drug addicts. On my last evening in Italy the big moment had come: I was going to propose to Mirjam. With my nerves raging, I took her to a chic restaurant. We had both dressed up nicely for a romantic evening out. The restaurant looked beautiful, with fountains and palm trees, but it turned out to be closed! I quickly ran back to our taxi driver and asked him to find another restaurant. It was already past eight o'clock and at ten o'clock all restaurants would be closed. And it had to happen that evening, because early the next day I would be returning to the Netherlands. We searched and searched, but it seemed that all the restaurants were closed.

At a quarter past nine, our driver finally found a small local restaurant which was open in one of Naples' back streets. We ran in. It was an old-fashioned, noisy place with live music blasting out and loads of people in jeans and T-shirts. We really stood out in our smart clothes. But I didn't care; I wanted to marry Mirjam. In my nervousness I ordered fish, although I prefer to eat meat, and I was trembling all over. Mirjam asked, "Are you okay? Would you like some water?"

Because of the loud music we could hardly hear each other, so when I saw that there was a small balcony with a neatly set table where it was a bit quieter, I suggested sitting there. Then it finally happened: I gave her the teddy bear, went down on my knees, and asked her if she would marry me. And she said yes! With tears in my eyes I put the ring on her finger and we kissed each other. We so much wanted to share our lives.

The next day, back in the Netherlands, I told my parents that Mirjam and I wanted to get married. They were very happy for us, but worried at the same time. My father said that first I had to save some money and find a permanent job so that I could take care of my wife. I was willing to do that, but I wanted even more to marry Mirjam quickly, so she would really be mine.

When Mirjam returned a month later, I got ready to arrange the wedding. But then Mirjam said, "I have spoken with the pastor's wife in Italy. She said that you can't just start a marriage. You must be financially strong, but also spiritually. You have a job and a car, but you haven't progressed spiritually in recent months." And then she said this, "It would be really good for you to go to Italy for six months." I was stunned. Mirjam had just returned, I had missed her for half a year, and now she wanted me to go away too? So we would not see each other for another six months? I wasn't sure about that. At the same time, I knew that the time I had spent in Amsterdam alone had not been a period of spiritual growth. Maybe I could come closer to God by leaving Amsterdam...

In the following weeks I talked a lot with Mirjam and God about a trip to Italy. Three months later I decided to go. I came home, went to my room, and prayed, "Lord, I don't know what You want, but I want to obey You. Do with me what You want." At that moment I knew that God was taking me on a journey of change. I called the pastor in Naples and told him I wanted to take time out and help them as a missionary among drug addicts. I was immediately welcomed.

Mirjam, my brother, Emiliano, and my parents took me to Schiphol. It was the first time since our return from America that I had left Amsterdam for a prolonged period. I was tense, but I tried to keep myself together. Mirjam embraced me and spoke encouraging words to me. She believed that I could do it and that God would be with me. I also believed that.

As the plane took off, tears were running down my cheeks. So much was going through my mind: my old street life, my conversion, my plan to marry Mirjam, God's plan for my life... I felt very lonely.

At the airport in Naples, I was picked up by Fernie, a big, friendly man whom I had met when I was visiting Mirjam. He showed me my bed in what used to be the garage of the house, between the beds of drug addicts who were living there. Every morning I had to get up at five o'clock, brush my teeth, and pray for an hour in the living room. Then, like all the others, I got to do my household chores: mopping the floor, vacuuming, cleaning the kitchen, or washing the pastor's car. After breakfast I had five minutes to take a shower and then we went out on the streets to evangelize. Throughout the day we told people about Jesus. On return home there was Bible study again.

I spent a lot of time with Fernie. We both liked music so we sang together and played guitar. We had a lot of fun, but we often prayed together as well. Fernie invested much time in me and became a kind of father figure to me.

I also prayed a lot in my room. Particularly on holidays, when the other guys went to see their families, I felt lonely and missed my family and Mirjam. At those moments I looked for God and I prayed on my knees. God began to reveal Himself to me: I received revelations, visions, and dreams about people in the house. I saw that God wanted to use me. In Italy, God separated me completely from my old, immoral life in Amsterdam. Here God seemed to look after me personally and my process of change was completed.

One place where we often evangelized was called The Bronx. There were many drug addicts there whom we could tell about Jesus and the new life He wants to give. One day I came across Sinanie from Tanzania. He was in Italy illegally and had been addicted to drugs for years. He was very skinny, had holes in his clothes, and looked like he hadn't had a shower for weeks. "Please, can you help me?" he asked me with despair in his voice.

I felt such a compassion for him that I simply couldn't leave him behind on his own. I asked Fernie to take Sinanie home, but there was no room in the bus. However, Fernie gave me a folder about the house, with the address on it. I passed it on to Sinanie, and he said he would certainly come because he really needed help. I prayed with him and went back with the bus. But after that I could not sleep, eat, or drink. I was constantly praying for Sinanie; it was a mission God had given me.

For two days I kept praying for Sinanie. Meanwhile, the work went on as usual, so I was busy cleaning the church when I heard the doorbell ring. A few moments later Fernie called to me. Next to him stood Sinanie, with his torn jacket, holes in his pants and shoes, and rotten teeth, but ripe and ready for a new life! I could pray the sinner's prayer with him.

Fernie was also pleased that Sinanie had arrived. I asked him to provide a place for this new brother to sleep, but the answer didn't make me happy: I had to give him my bed! Fernie told me I could sleep on the floor. In this way, he taught me to make sacrifices for the people of the street.

Sinanie had to go cold turkey to get off the drugs. For nights in a row he would vomit. I took care of him, made tea for him, and prayed with him. I did not get any rest, but I was delighted to see Sinanie slowly recovering. He started eating, he gained some weight, and decided to shave off his dreadlocks. He wanted to serve Jesus, although he had nothing.

The Lord spoke clearly to my heart about giving him some of my stuff. I was very attached to my belongings, especially my clothes. But Sinanie had nothing. With some effort, I gave him my beautiful black Prada slippers, which I liked a lot myself. But when I saw how grateful he was, I was happy too. Later, I also gave him my beautiful silk suit, which I had bought in Italy.

I had always put great value on clothes, but from then on God taught me not to see my outfit as an idol, but to use it to bless other people. I started to give my clothes to my housemates who came from the streets and didn't have anything. In Naples, I also learned to trust God. He took care of us. One day there was no more food in the house. For days we had eaten pasta with tomato sauce and dry bread. The pastor decided to pray and fast for twenty-four hours with the whole rehab team. We called out to God and asked Him to provide us with food and drink. The next morning we got a phone call: There was a truck on the way with pizzas, meat, bread, milk, and all we needed. Another time I went to the supermarket empty-handed. The supermarket manager then said that I could take as many groceries as I wanted. I went home with two big shopping bags, and shared everything with my roommates.

Meanwhile, I taught Sinanie everything I knew about the gospel. He drank it in. Years later, he called me to thank me for the time and energy I had invested in him. He told me that he had also become a preacher and was running a home for drug addicts. Together we thanked the Lord for His plan for Sinanie's life and for using me to get him out of the pit.

I had my drum kit sent to Naples, so I could play with the band in the church services. One day, a short, chubby twelve-year-old boy came up to me. He said, "Hi, I'm Giovanni; can you teach me to play drums?" I knew him a little: He had no father or brother, and no one who was really looking after him. In church he used to draw a lot of attention, often in a negative way. In fact, I found him quite an annoying kid, but I felt I had to teach him what I could because he had a great calling on his life.

Every day I gave Giovanni a lesson. I taught him all the basic techniques I knew. That was hard at times, because I often had to correct him. It wasn't easy to stay patient and sometimes I gave him a rough telling off, but he kept following me around. I also taught him to pray and read the Bible, and gradually started to really care about him. To him, I was like a big brother.

When I left to go back to the Netherlands, Giovanni began to cry. He was really sad because he would miss me. Years later, I heard that Giovanni had become a professional drummer. He is one of the most sought-after drummers among the evangelical congregations in Naples and also has students, just as he once was my student.

14 North Amsterdam

While I was in Italy, Mirjam and I communicated mainly through letters. Often I would be waiting for the postman, who came every afternoon around two o'clock. As soon as he arrived, I searched quickly through the stack of mail to see if there was a letter from Mirjam. In the evening I read all her letters again and I prayed a lot for our relationship.

When I returned to the Netherlands after seven months, Mirjam and I started working hard to prepare our wedding.

On the big day we had a fantastic party on an estate and a party ship, with hundreds of friends and relatives. After a nice, simple honeymoon we moved into our new house. It was an apartment consisting of a thirty-square-meter living room, a small kitchen, and a bedroom. We had to pay more than 900 euros a month for it. I worked for the minimum wage at Schiphol Airport while Mirjam had just graduated from college. She didn't have a job at her professional level yet, only a part-time job in a hotel. We weren't able to pay all the monthly bills and this caused a lot of stress. Mirjam did her best to make the most of it: Our old sofa was revamped with an IKEA cover and she created a cozy atmosphere, but in her eyes I saw the disappointment.

The first months of our marriage were anything but rosy. We had a lot of arguments. We shouted at each other and I hit holes in the walls and doors. Fortunately, I never hit Mirjam, but sometimes the arguments were so fierce that the police came around. Mirjam camouflaged the holes in the walls with picture frames and other solutions so our guests couldn't see anything. We both doubted the wisdom of getting married and lacked good counsel and guidance. For Mirjam, it was difficult to allow a man in her life: She had grown up with her single mother and had no contact with her father, so she had no example of a good marriage.

We asked the church leadership for help, but didn't get what we needed. We were told that we had to pray a lot and listen to each other well, but that wasn't enough for us. In hindsight we should have done a marriage course before we got married and we could have done with good guidance at the beginning of our marriage. Fortunately, God did not let go of us and He kept us together through all the problems and arguments. Our love for God and for each other was strong.

In the meantime we were working hard in the church. We led the worship, we helped in Sunday school, I led the youth, and sometimes we spoke to the church or led Bible studies. Much of our free time was taken up with God's work because we wanted to serve Him. Looking back, however, I think we could have worked better at our marriage. I was falling into the same trap as my father: I spent so much time working for God that I neglected my first responsibility, which was my family.

We did not just quarrel, we also prayed together. It was clear that our problems stemmed from the fact that we had too small a home, for which we were paying too much money. That's why we started praying and fasting a lot for a new and affordable house. We also searched the web for homes and mortgages that we could cope with. God heard our prayers: In 2003 we found a beautiful single-family home in an old neighborhood in North Amsterdam, which we could afford. Now peace and quiet were being restored our life.

However, God had not given us a house in North Amsterdam purely for that reason. We live in a nice street, but down the road are the less favored areas, the rough districts, with many young people who have few prospects. Many boys there grow up without a father and lack the support and guidance they need at home. From my own experience, I know what that means. Every day we heard the police sirens; every week there was a robbery or a shooting.

Miriam and I prayed together, asking God to show us what we could do for the youth in this area. I went to the pastor of our church and told him about the needs in North Amsterdam. He gave me his blessing to work for God in this area: I would get financial and practical support from the church. Then I started visiting the community centers, schools, district councils, and anyone who could help me to hire a room so I could reach young people who did not know Jesus. After days of conversation, I met the director of all community centers in North Amsterdam. I told him about my past and my heart for these lost youngsters. He listened to me willingly, and although he wasn't a believer himself, he gave me permission to use a small community center. "If it can make the youth better, why not?" he said.

Mirjam and I prayed for a theme for these evenings, and God gave us the theme of "The Gift." We wanted to tell young people that God gave us His Son Jesus as a gift. We made posters and flyers and distributed them to schools and throughout the neighborhood. I also mobilized all my friends who played gospel music to make sure we had good music during the evening. When the event finally took place, dozens of young people came to watch. Antillean, Surinamese, Turkish, and Moroccan boys heard my testimony. Many of them had the same background of loneliness, alcohol and drug abuse, and crime as I have.

We loved these evenings, and more and more young people started to come. I was also invited into schools to share my testimony. Soon, we were able to use a larger community center, and more and more people were helping to fill the program. The young people began to recognize me: When I went shopping, the boys on the street would call out, "Hey, Street Preacher, when are you going to organize another evening?"

Dozens of young people were coming to the evening events, but when we moved to a larger neighborhood I started praying even more for a big harvest of young people from the street. Long before the next event started one evening there was a long queue in front of the entrance to the community center. That night there weren't dozens but four hundred young people who came to take part! We started with music to worship Jesus and show that gospel music is not boring: There was rap and breakdancing by some of the Christian youth I knew from the church. Finally, I went up and preached about the Good Samaritan. Then I made an altar call and dozens of young people came forward, many of whom gave their lives to Jesus. Some of them I picked up on Sunday to take them to church. Although the pastors didn't really know how to deal with them, I thought it important to bring them to church.

15 OLD FRIENDS

With my marriage and our new calling in North Amsterdam, my life had got a clearer direction. In our new home we had more space, and also more financial security. I spent a lot of time making music for God as part of a live band which I formed with my good friend and bass player Raoel. We played almost every weekend in churches, at Christian weddings, and on other occasions. But then I heard that my old friend Howard wasn't doing so well. He had psychological problems and even suffered from psychosis. I started searching for him. Eventually I found him and invited him to my house. Our new home still needed a lot of decorating and he wanted to help me put up wallpaper. It was like the days of old: We had a lot of fun and loads to talk about. When I brought him home, I said to him, "Howard, you know that Jesus loves you, don't you?" He confirmed that, and told me that he really wanted to change and be healed. I could pray with him and bless him. We embraced each other and he asked, "Do you want to forgive me?" I did not understand him: What did I have to forgive him for? "Everything," he said. "Forgive me, okay, Jay?" He said goodbye and went back home.

Two weeks later I received a phone call: Howard had jumped in front of a train.

I was dumbfounded. There were dozens of people at his funeral. I had to say something about our friendship, but I couldn't understand or accept that Howard's life had had to end this way. It took me a year to get over the worst of it. At the same time, Howard's death motivated me to win as many youngsters as possible for Jesus.

I was serving God with my music and by organizing youth events, but it didn't seem enough. Mirjam and I wanted to do more for God, but that wasn't possible within the church we were members of. That's why we decided to go to another church to hear God's voice. For two years we visited a church where God's Word was preached in a clear and good way, but where I also started to get bored. Until we had a meal on Christmas Day with the whole church. It was cozy and there was a lot of food, way too much. After the meal they wanted to throw away the remaining food, but God told me I had to share it with the addicts on the Zeedijk, in the city center. The pastor was enthusiastic about this idea and gave me all the food. Mirjam and I drove to the Zeedijk. I asked Mirjam to stay in the car and pray for me. I took out the boxes of food and divided them among the dozens of addicts who were hanging around there. Meanwhile, I told them about Jesus.

There, at that very moment, I knew that God would use us and that He had a specific calling for Mirjam and me.

A few months later I was praying. I knew that God had a calling for us, but I didn't know exactly what that calling was and how we could put it into action. I asked, "Lord, what do You want me to do for You? Is there something more I can do?" Then I fell asleep and dreamed that I was in a big church with my parents and Mirjam. My mother pointed to us and said, "Joshua and Mirjam are the pastors, not us." Then I woke up.

I had mixed feelings because I enjoyed my life as a musician, but it seemed that I had to become a pastor. I said, "Lord, do You want me to be a pastor?" From that day on, I couldn't forget about this dream. God even gave me a desire for it. I had just one big problem: Mirjam couldn't see herself as a pastor's wife at all. We used to joke about it, and on that point she was always very determined: She did not want to be married to a pastor. That's why I said, "Lord, if it's Your will, let me see a change in this too. Let Mirjam respond positively."

When I came home, I told Mirjam that God had spoken to me and said that I was to be a pastor. Slightly anxious, I waited for her response. Miriam said calmly, "This might sound crazy, Josh, but lately I've been thinking about this!" She was positive! We prayed together.

I talked to my pastor, but he wasn't very encouraging. He told me that I first had to go to a Bible college. I was willing to do that, but also wanted to get straightforward practical training. In our church that wasn't available, so we started by ourselves. Mirjam advised me, however, to get some training first from a church or faith organization, but I was in a hurry because I felt the pressure of my calling. I forgot that time and patience are needed.

I had a vision to win the world for God and I couldn't wait. We therefore called our church "Worldwide Vision Ministries." At first we only held Bible studies at our home, under the guidance of my parents. After a few months we rented a building in South Amsterdam, where we held our services on Sundays, but it didn't work out the way we were hoping. There weren't many people coming to the services, and we didn't see people becoming believers either. We moved to another location, but that didn't work either. That's why we decided to go back to the basics: We started having Sunday services at home again. At first there were about ten people, but soon it grew to thirty or more. We got people with addiction problems, teenage mothers, youths with social issues; in short: the weakest in our society.

Apart from doing the church ministry, I worked part-time for an agency. Miriam had a job at the EO (Evangelical Broadcasting company). Pretty soon after this she became pregnant with our first child and we had a daughter, Neviah. We were happy to have her and I was looking forward to becoming the best father I could think of. I would spend a lot of time with our kids and give them everything I had missed myself. One and a half years later, our son Santino was born and I was jumping with joy. I had really wanted a son! During the whole pregnancy, I had believed that God would give me a son and here he was! I was looking forward to building our father–son relationship and showing him how important he was to me. I didn't know that I would have another son seven years later, Kisar.

At that time, we decided to hire a room again for our church services. We found one in the center of Amsterdam, near Central Station. The church continued to grow, with up to seventy people.

I regularly spoke during street rallies (evangelization campaigns) in Belgium. Once I stood on the street underneath a canvas roof, speaking about people who had given their lives to God. Mirjam saw a strong wind blowing over the tent, and we knew it was the power of the Holy Spirit. I was also invited to Naples to speak in churches and at youth meetings. Meanwhile, the ministry in the Netherlands was moving on as well. Together with Mirjam, my parents, brother, sister, and other Christians, we built up the church: We evangelized on the streets, among tourists and other passersby, and we shared food among homeless people and told them about Jesus.

This work can't be done without prayer, so we held regular prayer meetings. During one of those meetings at home with my parents I heard a trauma helicopter flying over the house. There were also many police cars going back and forth. I went out to see what was going on. The police had put up a white tent and a large part of the street was closed off. I saw some old friends, who were crying. Two people had been shot. It turned out to be Iron Mike, the youngest brother of Ponky, my old buddy, and his friend Lotje. Fortunately, they hadn't died, but were taken to the hospital in a critical condition. I went straight to the hospital, where I met the family. We weren't allowed in. The doctors had said that Iron Mike had little chance of survival, but I asked his family if I could pray with them and they agreed. I asked God to save his life and give him one more chance. God answered that prayer: Days later, I heard that Iron Mike had survived this crisis. A few weeks later, however, he died from an infection. I had to lead the funeral service.

In the following days, I encountered more friends and acquaintances from earlier times, and whenever I got the opportunity I told them about Jesus. I met Clifton, my former arch enemy. He told me that he had been jailed for five years because he had shot someone, but that he was now the proud father of a son. He also said he was sorry for the fight we had had in the past. I told him that I had changed and that Jesus had come into my life. He was interested and I was able to tell him more about my faith. Months later, I heard that he had died of cancer. How glad I was that I had been able to tell him about Jesus!

On one occasion I was evangelizing in the Warmoesstraat (in the center of Amsterdam) when I saw a familiar face. It was Boneka. I knew him from the past, when we used to hang out together and we had also fought once. Recently, he had been portrayed in the media as one of the top criminals of South Amsterdam. I walked up to him and gave him a flyer from our church. He recognized me immediately. I told him that I had seen a lot about him in the media, but that I was now serving Jesus and that he should do the same. He grinned and said, "Good luck, gap. I know what you were like and I'm glad you have changed." Then he walked off quickly. From that day on I prayed for him, that he would listen to Jesus' invitation. A few weeks later I saw in the news that Boneka had died together with a friend during a liquidation in Leiderdorp, a nearby town. Another friend from the past had lost his life. My heart hurt.

I went to his funeral and saw many acquaintances from the underworld. A tall guy came towards me and said, "Josh! Do you remember me? Quincy Soetersonojo van Gein! I was so small then and always looked up to you, man!" I was happy to see him, but Quincy's life was already going downhill. A while later I encountered him again. He had joined the Satudarah motorcycle club and the Crips Gang (in Amsterdam). He had tattoos all over his face and body and he had been in jail for a while.

I was worried about Quincy and told him about the gospel. I said, "Jesus wants your life. Give it to Him now, because tomorrow it might no longer be possible." I talked to him for a quarter of an hour, but he kept saying," I have other thoughts about faith," or "Hey, I will be fine." Not long after that he was shot in South-East Amsterdam. He got six bullets in the chest and did not survive.

Deeply saddened, I contacted his mother and asked her if I could say something at the funeral. I knew there would be hundreds of "Quincys" who all needed the gospel. His mother agreed. At the funeral there were many members of the motorcycle club and the Crips Gang. I was called forward and spoke on Matthew 27:38, the passage about Jesus hanging on the cross between two criminals. Jesus was merciful to the one who asked Him for mercy. He also wants to show His mercy to young people today. Afterwards, several Crips Gang members and members of the motorcycle club came to me to express their appreciation for the sermon I had given. Once again, I was able to sow the word of God.

Unfortunately, this wasn't the last time I spoke at the funeral of a young criminal. When I worked as a youth leader, I had got to know young Eaneas Lomp. Initially he came to church regularly, but later he drifted away. He entered the criminal world with the boys from West Amsterdam. His name appeared in the media several times; he was suspected of involvement in liquidations. I tried to contact him through family members and friends, but nobody knew how to get in touch with him. In 2015 I heard from other people that he was in prison. I got the address of the prison where he was in custody, and wrote him a long, encouraging letter telling him that God wanted to help him. I didn't get a reply.

At the beginning of October I was in a parking lot in North Amsterdam when I heard someone calling my name several times. I turned around and saw a bodybuilder type of guy running towards me; it was Eaneas! He told me he had received my letter, but that he had not responded because the media were continuously after him. He also said his name was on a hit list, so his life could be over any time. I told him, "God wants to help you now. There's no guarantee of tomorrow." I urged him to give his life to Jesus right away. There were tears in his eyes as we hugged each other, and then he disappeared again. A few weeks later, I heard that he had been liquidated. I was allowed to speak during his farewell service, and dozens of youngsters from Amsterdam's underworld heard the message of Jesus.

16 A NEW LIFE

Over the last twenty years I've learned a lot. For the first four or five years I was looking for my identity as a Christian. I was very young when I accepted Jesus and temptations like alcohol, drugs, and cigarettes were everywhere. It would have been easier for me if I had been sent to a Bible school abroad, where I could have grown in my faith and become stronger as a Christian. However, that didn't happen, and in the beginning it took a lot of effort for me to make radical choices.

Now, twenty years later, I can thankfully say that I have no desire to go back to cigarettes, drugs, or alcohol. I have received blessings which I would never have had without Jesus: my salvation, my family life, church life, and more. I no longer struggle with aggression and I give as much time and attention as possible to my family. Every day, I enjoy the small and big things I experience with my children: having breakfast together, taking them to school, having conversations and cuddles, putting the children to bed, enjoying wonderful holidays together every year, and, above all, telling them about God, praying with them, and attending church as a family.

In my daily life I try to find a good balance between God, family, and work. I usually get up before our children are awake. I quietly make a cup of coffee, get dressed, and take time to pray and read the Bible. For me, talking to God is the most important thing at the beginning of each day. Then we make breakfast for the children and Mirjam and I pray together before she goes to work. When she's working I take the kids to school; when she is free, Mirjam does it. Before we leave, we pray with the children. Our house is within cycling distance of the school. During the bike rides, we often have the best conversations.

Once the children are at school, I cycle straight to the church office. There the work begins: appointments, home visits to church members, training sessions (discipleship) with young people from church, visiting people in hospital and praying for or with them. Quite regularly I have the opportunity to share my testimony in a television or radio program.

Of course, I also use this time to prepare my sermons and meet with the church leadership team or with other pastors in our region. Besides all of this church ministry, I'm working with PreLev, a prevention project which provides advice and life-skill training in schools and youth prisons. A few times a year I travel abroad for speaking engagements and quite often I share my life story in churches and youth groups and at conferences.

My work is different from a nine-to-five job, especially because unexpected things often happen. But, no matter how busy we are, Mirjam and I make sure that twice a week we sit around the dining table as a family for at least two hours. Mirjam cooks special, yummy food and we take a lot of time to talk, pray, and play (Bible) games. We have a prayer book in which we write down our prayer requests, including those of the children. For example, Santino prays for my sister's daughter, and Neviah prays that Dad and Mom will always be in love with each other.

Every Saturday we take time to relax and chill; we spend time as a family and don't do any church ministry. We go for a walk together, watch a movie, or bake pancakes at home. Our older son Santino is now seven years old and plays soccer; I am the trainer of his team, which also creates a close relationship between the two of us.

Every year we go on a family holiday somewhere in Europe. We make sure that we really have a time-out. We even leave our mobile phones at home; we just take a simple device for emergency calls. During those weeks we have time only for God and our family.

I have learned that God is number one, but that family goes before church. There is a difference between God and God's work. People sometimes think that "working for God" is the same as having a relationship with Him. I always try to be aware of this fact: My first priority is to build my relationship with God and my family; church ministry comes after that.

Nowadays I also have a good relationship with my father. We not only connect in our work for God, but we are also "truly" father and son.

Epilogue by Ferry Kotadiny

"Grandchildren are the crowning glory of the aged; parents are the pride of their children."
Proverbs 17:6 (NLT)

I thank God for His love, mercy, and faithfulness, and for the fact that all of my children and grandchildren are following and serving Jesus Christ, together with me and my wife. In this book you have read how God turned my son Joshua from someone who was always stumbling and failing in life into someone who has a significant and positive influence on his environment. Joshua and his wife, Mirjam, are blessed pastors in the church and loving parents to their family. They aren't perfect but do their utmost to follow God's will.

This book is a wake-up call for all parents who want to walk according to God's Word (the Bible) and be led by the Holy Spirit. Jesus said, "You will know a tree by its fruit." Your family – spouse and children – are to be number one. Because, when your family is unstable, you will suffer emotional damage. Your mind-set and spiritual life won't be the way they should, and you won't be able to have a positive impact on your environment.

To all fathers I want to say this: If you have maybe failed in this regard, it is important to face your shortcomings. It starts with confronting yourself and then you need to confess and ask the Lord Jesus for forgiveness. Then you need to truly repent of all wrong decisions, thoughts, and behavior (by letting go of them and unlearning them). Those around you, especially your wife, children, and grandchildren, must be able to notice a real and positive change in your life (fruit). Your family is an important part of the community; in fact, it is a cornerstone.

Based on my own experience I can truly say: Apply these life principles and go for gold – nothing less.

The one and only Ferry Kotadiny

Acknowledgements

I would like to thank those who are important in my life and those who have contributed to this book.

First of all, I thank Jesus Christ, my Savior and Redeemer. When I look back on my wild teenage years and see how most of my old friends have ended up (addicted, in prison, or even murdered), I thank God for His grace in my life. I have ended up well and I am now living with a purpose, which is to serve God. I know I could have gone down the same road as my former friends.

Second, I want to thank my wife, Mirjam, for believing in me and the vision God gave me, even after fourteen years of marriage, in which we have shared beautiful but also difficult moments:

You are so special to me and I love having you with me. You are my pride, my blessing, and my haven. You are the love of my life and also my soul mate; without you I don't feel complete. Whenever we are together, whether it is for ministry or in private, I feel strength. I believe this is the strength of unity!

I want to thank my children, Neviah, Santino, and Kisar, because you always remind Daddy why I am doing all this. When I come home after a busy day, I feel the joy, blessing, and security of a loving family. It always reminds me of the fact that you are my first priority; my first and foremost ministry. Thank you for supporting Daddy's vision, which he received from God.

I can't thank my parents enough for all they have done for me. Dad, you always showed us that God's Word had the final authority in our family. Through all the highs and lows we have been through in our lives, you have always held on to God. You are my hero and you still are my example.

Mom, thank you for showing your children the power of prayer. I still regret causing you so much heartache as a street boy. However, you did not allow me to become lost but persevered in prayer so that now I can live for God. I promise that, wherever I preach, I will mention you as an example which shows the power of a mother who prays for her son.

I am very grateful to my brother, Emiliano, as well. Even if you didn't realize it at the time, God was working through you when you invited me to the youth camp where Jesus saved me.

Ravenna and Alvah, my sister and niece, thank you for being part of my family. You have seen me change from a young troublemaker into a pastor. I know you've always been praying for me. Thank you for that!

I thank those who supported Mirjam and me in our relationship:

Howard: Although his life had a bad ending, I will always be grateful for his friendship and for the way he encouraged me to choose Mirjam as my spouse for life.

Marja, Mirjam's sister, who, from the first day we met, wanted to see Mirjam and me get together. Thanks to your funny remarks and quiet hints and suggestions, Mirjam and I are now truly together.

Thanks again to my parents and to my mother-in-law (Ilse Kortzorg) for guiding us according to biblical principles during our courtship.

To my publisher, Gerhard Rijksen at Gideon, thank you for publishing this book and for your ongoing efforts to spread the gospel within this country and around the world.

I also want to thank Willeke, the editor of this book. You and I come from completely different backgrounds and you have never had anything to do with street life. However, I am impressed by the way you have managed to edit the story and make it sound as if you are familiar with this lifestyle. In Amsterdam we would say: "Your work is toppie!"

A thank-you also goes to all the pastors who believe in this book and my story and who recommend the book in order to reach many families, and especially lost youth. Together, as one body, we are strong.

Finally, I want to thank all of the people from Worldwide Vision Church, of which I am the senior pastor. You have continuously prayed for this project and the church supports the calling God has given to me and Mirjam. Let us reach this target group and those living in need across the world with the gospel!

Printed in Great Britain
by Amazon

Finding Grace
in the Gutter